Endorsements

Pastor Rick Ciaramitaro is one of the most thankful people I know. He is also one of the most fruitful pastors I know. I believe thankfulness is a prerequisite to fruitfulness. This book is an excellent opportunity to learn from someone who practices what he preaches about thankfulness.

—Pastor Mark Hazzard
Senior Pastor, Parkwood Gospel Temple
Windsor, Ontario

Ready to be refreshed? In need of discovering the secret to contentment, happiness, and joy? In one word, *The Secret to Kingdom Life* will unlock for you the key to a full, *yes overflowing*, life in Christ. Read this book now; you need it.

—Dr. Larry Keefauver, President YMCS
Best-selling Author and International Teacher

Pastor Rick is one of the most gratefully generous people I know! He lives what he teaches, and I've been a benefactor of his kingdom-mindedness on many occasions.

—Dr. Garth Leno
Pastor, Heritage Park Alliance Church
Windsor, Ontario

Clive Barker once said, "Everybody is a book of blood. When we're opened, we're read." The pages of *The Secret to Kingdom Life* are stained with the blood, sweat, and tears of a pastor/leader who has paid the high price of guarding his heart with gratitude and outrageous generosity over decades of ministry. In doing so, Rick has found the secret to a fruitful and full life. Rick has left his heart on the pages of this book. I highly endorse it, because I highly esteem and endorse him. Open it and be read by the Author and Finisher of our Faith.

—Brad Watson, Lead Pastor
Lakeshore St. Andrew's Presbyterian Church
Tecumseh, Ontario

Pastor Rick nails it when he delivers the keys to longevity in the Kingdom; it's even better watching him practice it every day.

—RJ Ciaramitaro
Associate Pastor WCF

The Secret to Kingdom Life is not really a secret! Throughout the Old and New Testaments God repeatedly revealed the key to accessing the fullness of His power and goodness, yet so many people have missed it. Rick skillfully points the way to living in the abundance of His great blessings. Read it; let it transform your thinking, and you'll discover an exciting new and supernatural way of living!

—Bill Prankard

The Secret to Kingdom Life

Rick Ciaramitaro

The Secret to Kingdom Life

© 2011 Rick Ciaramitaro

ISBN: 978-1-937514-12-9

Camden House Books, LLC.
Tulsa, Oklahoma

Printed in Canada

Dedication

Two people have profoundly impacted my life in the most incredible ways. I would like to dedicate this book to the both of them. Number one is my Lord and Savior Jesus Christ. He has been totally amazing to me these last thirty-eight years. Jesus has been so very faithful to me, my family, and ministry He has entrusted to me. I am so appreciative today for the work of the Cross that He revealed to us of His plan, purpose, and destiny for each of us on the planet, and by His grace I will serve Him the rest of my life.

The second person I dedicate this book to is my wife, Cathy, who has been an amazing encouragement, strength, and blessing to my life. Her dedication to preaching the Cross of Christ has impacted me incredibly. I am so thankful that the two of us have been called by God for such a time as this in His Kingdom.

Acknowledgments

I would like to acknowledge my staff and members at Windsor Christian Fellowship, who have been so amazingly loyal, committed, and dedicated to the cause of Christ. Together they have had an incredible passion to reach lost, wavering, and hurting people with the love, hope, and answer to fallen mankind, which is Christ.

The saints at WCF have caused such a heart of gratitude to come forth from my life as each one of the members has taken seriously the mandate on their life to connect to the Lord and to one another. I have never seen such caring, dedicated, and devoted disciples of Jesus anywhere in all my travels. I am so grateful that I have been entrusted with the oversight of the greatest people on the planet, who take great delight in living for and serving our King.

Table of Contents

Foreword by George Woodward............................ xi

Introduction   God's Secret Just for You! xiii

Chapter 1   Atmosphere in the Spirit World 19

Chapter 2   Keys to Being in the Will
            of God 31

Chapter 3   Keys to Releasing God's Glory
            in the Earth...................................49

Chapter 4   Thanksgiving in Psalms.................57

Chapter 5   Thanksgiving in Prayer..................69

Chapter 6   Thanksgiving Brings Restoration
            and Health....................................81

Chapter 7   The Destruction Caused by
            Murmuring and Complaining 87

Chapter 8   Breaking Out of Complacency
            and Ingratitude 97

Chapter 9   Thanksgiving in Communion 115

Final Word   Live Thanksgiving 123

About the Author...127

Other Books by Rick Ciaramitaro.......................129

Endnotes..131

Foreword

Character, longevity, purpose, and fruitfulness are some of the many attributes that describe the man, Rick Ciaramitaro. He has a pastor's heart and an apostolic call for his family, his church, his city, and his nation. When he writes, you quickly sense the voice of the Holy Spirit echoing from the pages.

I believe Rick is called to bring reconciliation and restoration to the Body of Christ in these last days. Unity is still one of the major roadblocks today, but if we can embrace the fundamental truth of this book, it will take us much further along that road.

Today there is much discussion and focus on the teaching of Jesus when His disciples asked Him how to pray. One of the things He taught them was to pray for God's Kingdom to come. The fundamental truth of this book—thanksgiving—is a major building block of His Kingdom. It is a pillar that will change and then uphold your life as you make it a part of who you genuinely are.

As you explore the pages of this book, you will experience God's presence, learn His will for you, solve problems, create unity, weather storms, and find healing for your body. As you incorporate thankfulness into your life, it has the power to change everything.

I wholeheartedly recommend this book to you. It is not complicated but it is very profound. I believe this truth will revolutionize your life if you will embrace it.

—George Woodward,
Israel's Peace Ministries

INTRODUCTION

God's Secret Just for You!

I *want to share the secret of God's Kingdom life* *with you!* Jesus taught His disciples in the Book of Acts about things pertaining to the Kingdom of God. The Kingdom was the last teaching that He shared with the disciples before He ascended into Heaven. Apparently He felt it was so important that He drilled it into them for forty solid days. This book is about releasing the Kingdom life that Christ purchased for us at Calvary's Cross.

Living in the Kingdom is a powerful force against the enemy, the flesh, and the influence of the world that we all live in. Many believers never attain even a simple understanding of what Kingdom life is. Many have made the Kingdom life such a complicated, mysterious journey that few ever connect to it.

I have found the secret to entering and main- *taining the Kingdom life. I truly believe that* *what I am sharing in this book will put you on a journey of faith that will lead you into living the Kingdom life.*

In the last thirty-eight years, I have functioned as a father, grandfather, mentor, pastor, and some even call me a spiritual father in Canada. I have seen many men and women of God who have everything going for them suddenly lose their steam. They seemed to be experiencing everything they had ever dreamed of: incredible blessings, powerful break-through, strong anointing, and growth in their ministries. Then they gradually begin to let down their guard until they get pulled into some form of deception, weird teaching, bondage, sin, or work of the flesh. Their ministries begin to spiral down and their influence begins to wane. I have asked the Lord why so many have not finished well and have read many books on the subject. I have agonized in prayer over this same scenario many times and asked the Holy Spirit to help me finish well the ministry entrusted to my life so that the generations to come would follow in the right ways of the Lord.

Over many years of studying the Scriptures, I believe I have found the missing key for longevity in ministry and for the fulfillment of prophetic words from many years ago. This study has also shown me why, at times, God's presence and power seem to be very distant from our lives and our prayers; intercession and crying out does not get the answers that we are believing for by faith. By His grace, I believe this book will answer the WHY. It is a very simple truth and maybe that is why so few have found the secret. The key to unlocking Kingdom life is *thanks-giving*. Through this book you will see a key symbol ⌐, which will be a key to unlock a wonderful secret about thanksgiving in your walk with the Lord. Read it. Say it out loud. Memorize it and then live it!

⌐ The key to Kingdom living is gratitude; it is a heart of thanksgiving.

Because you did not serve the Lord your God with joy and gladness of heart, for the abundance of everything, therefore you shall serve your enemies, whom the Lord will send against you, in hunger, in thirst, in naked-ness, and in need of everything; and He will put a yoke of iron on your neck until He has destroyed you. (Deuteronomy 28:47-48)

There it is; the answer is right there in the Bible. When someone asks us "why," we say, "because...." The word "because" is used 1,477 times in the Word of God and means *for this reason, due to the fact that*. In the verse above, the fact was they were ungrateful for and had begun to take for granted the blessings of God in their lives. They had started to murmur and complain, which are symptoms of lost joy. They did not appreciate what God had done so He stopped blessing them.

This same thing seems to be happening in many churches today. A pastor serves and pours his life into them by teaching and modeling the Christian life. He connects people to small groups, provides them with rides to church, and sees they receive help paying their utility bills. He counsels their families, helps their marriages, buries their loved ones, and performs their children's weddings. Then one day these same people get upset with something that is usually a petty offense or a misunderstanding and they leave. They totally disconnect from the church family that loved them and made sacrifices for them.

Many people come to the House of the Lord and take everything they can get from it and never return the least amount of gratitude. This type of behavior describes a parasite which takes and takes but never gives anything back. They take the most valuable nutrients of the food that comes into the body and leave the leftovers for the rest to eat. Parasites are so selfish they only concern themselves with their desires and make it tough for the rest of the body to function. When parasites are in a church the rest of the body has to work harder to keep the energy level up and constantly guard themselves from broken focus, fatigue, and burn out.

One of the main characteristics of the end-times is the spirit of anti-Christ that is sent to wear down the saints. That's exactly what ingratitude does. It tires out the ministers and zaps the congregation of its passion and fervency for evangelism by forcing them to concentrate instead on putting out fires in the church. Many people pray for years that God would bring a husband or a wife into their lives. Then they find mister or miss right and get married. Six months later they want to divorce them. What happened? They became ungrateful for the blessing God brought into their lives. We see this with older couples who have been married as many years as I am old. They start running around on their spouse or leave them for a much younger man or women they've met in some online chat room. What happened? They became discontented, started taking their mate for granted, lost sight of their appreciation and vow, and became cold in their hearts over the process of time. Thanksgiving will keep the fire burning in every marriage.

It's the same thing with children. When they are growing up, Mom and Dad sacrifice their time, money, cars, savings, and energy to help their children through school. Then they run them all over town as a glorified taxi service so they can participate in all kinds of activities and sports. They cook decent meals, make lunches, wash clothes, clean up after them, and generally make sure they have the essentials of life. Parents buy them clothes, computers, and cell phones trying to help them in any way they can to get a good start on their independent life in the future. But oftentimes the children move out of the home and forget about Mom and Dad. They hardly ever call them, visit them, or even remember their birthdays, anniversaries, Mother's Day or Father's Day. But when Mom or Dad dies, they are the first ones there to get the inheritance. That's the fruit of being ungrateful.

Many parents don't expect a whole lot from their children after they move out of the house, but children must respect their parents. The Bible says children are to treat parents with honor for the blessing of God to be on their life, as well as to live a long life.[1] The truths you are about to learn in this book are from forty years of observation, studying people, and the Word of God. I pray you will enjoy learning **_The Secret to Kingdom Life_**.

CHAPTER 1

Atmosphere in the Spirit World

I learned as a young believer many years ago that there are atmospheres—certain scents, fragrances, or aromas that surround a believer's life, whether positive or negative. Second Corinthians 2:14-16 reads, "But thanks be to God, who always leads us in triumphal procession in Christ and through us spreads everywhere the fragrance of the knowledge of him. For we are to God the aroma of Christ among those who are being saved and those who are perishing. To the one we are the smell of death; to the other, the fragrance of life."

Thanksgiving's scented aroma filling the atmosphere of a believer's life attracts the Holy Spirit just as constant negativity and murmuring attracts the demonic realm into your life. I remember a time when I was greatly burdened by a betrayal that had taken place in my life several years before, and little to my understanding at the time I opened the door for arthritis to come into my arms as a result of not properly dealing with it through the Cross of Christ and His forgiveness. I learned that I had mentally assented to the need for forgivingness related to those who had betrayed me, but I didn't have a heart conviction to forgive. I believe there are many believers today who mentally assent to forgiving someone, but every time their name or the situation comes up to us, it's just as if what happened was happening all over again.

I remember speaking the Scriptures over my circumstance, yet nothing was changing, and the pain of just trying to hold my Bible up while preaching the Word of God was incredible. One morning before I left for church I totally left all my burdens at the altar in my prayer time and I confessed to the Lord that what had gotten inside of my heart was very ugly. I felt like a two-ton weight had lifted off me, but still had the pain in my arms. When I entered into church that morning and began to worship and thank the Lord for all He had done for my life, I started to weep and could not stop weeping. My heart was releasing more and more hurt as I experienced God's love in a powerful way.

The atmosphere was incredible as the congregation continued to worship, and I remember that lifting my hands up was very difficult to do. But as I surrendered, I was healed that very moment, and I have played tennis and done many other activities that I could not do before. I have walked in my healing to this day. I learned that morning that when the atmosphere is cleansed through thanksgiving and worship, then the Holy Spirit can accomplish His work in our lives. This is why the entry point of coming into His presence is always led by thanksgiving. Since that day I try to remember daily that the atmosphere that is accommodating for the Holy Spirit is gratitude. My life has not been the same since this revelation came.

King David understood the atmosphere of thanksgiving. In the Bible, King David was known as a worshipper, a lover, a writer of many psalms, Israel's greatest King, and as a man after God's own heart. In 1 Chronicles 16:1-7, we see how David followed the pattern given to create the atmosphere for inviting in the Presence of God.

*So they brought the ark of God, and set it in the midst of the tabernacle that David had erected for it. Then they offered burnt offerings and peace offerings before God. And when David had finished offering the burnt offerings and the peace offerings, he blessed the people in the name of the Lord. Then he distributed to everyone of Israel, both man and woman, to everyone a loaf of bread, a piece of meat, and a cake of raisins. **And he appointed some of the Levites to minister before the ark of the Lord, to commemorate, to thank, and to praise the Lord God of Israel:** Asaph the chief, and next to him Zechariah, then Jeiel, Shemiramoth, Jehiel, Mattithiah, Eliab, Benaiah, and Obed-Edom:*

Jeiel with stringed instruments and harps, but Asaph made music with cymbals; Benaiah and Jahaziel the priests regularly blew the trumpets before the ark of the covenant of God. On that day David first delivered this psalm into the hand of Asaph and his brethren, to thank the Lord: (emphasis added)

First, the Levites had a threefold work:

#1- to commemorate or bring to remembrance, recount, and record,
#2- to thank,
#3- to praise or to celebrate, shine, and rave about God.

Notice that right in the middle of recording and celebration is thanks. Then the text says on that day that the Ark of the Covenant was brought back to Israel, the first thing King David did was deliver a psalm to Asaph and his brethren to thank the Lord. David recognized a simple truth that was incredibly powerful and shows us that the first thing we need to do when we come before the Lord is be thankful.

This psalm of thanks that David brought is recorded in 1 Chronicles 16:8-10. "Oh, give thanks to the Lord! Call upon His name; Make known His deeds among the peoples! Sing to Him, sing psalms to Him; Talk of all His wondrous works! Glory in His holy name; Let the hearts of those rejoice who seek the Lord!" Notice that before the charge to "call on His Name" comes "the giving of thanks."

☛ Thanksgiving sanctifies the atmosphere for the Holy Spirit of God to move in.

Look in Psalm 100:4, "Enter into His gates with thanksgiving, And into His courts with praise. Be thankful to Him, and bless His name." The writer tells us to enter or go into His gates or His throne room with thanksgiving.

Then we see the praise and worship team is being assembled in 1 Chronicles 25:1-3:

Moreover David and the captains of the army separated for the service some of the sons of Asaph, of Heman, and of Jeduthun, who should prophesy with harps, stringed instruments, and cymbals. And the number of the skilled men performing their service was: Of the sons of Asaph: Zaccur, Joseph, Nethaniah, and Asharelah; the sons of Asaph were under the direction of Asaph, who prophesied according to the order of the king. Of Jeduthun, the sons of Jeduthun: Gedaliah, Zeri, Jeshaiah, Shimei, Hashabiah, and Mattithiah, six, under the direction of their father Jeduthun, who prophesied with a harp to give thanks and to praise the Lord.

Notice that this worship team is expanding and is now comprised of 288 trained and skilled worshipers in music for the Lord. Notice the authority and the pattern established for all worship leaders, choir directors, and minstrels. We can see that they were positioned for a visitation of the Lord's glory and it resulted when the atmosphere was charged with thanks and praise.

Now notice what happened when both teams under Asaph with the Levites came into unity and made one sound praising and thanking God:

*And it came to pass when the priests came out of the Most Holy Place (for all the priests who were present had sanctified themselves, without keeping to their divisions), and the Levites who were the singers, all those of Asaph and Heman and Jeduthun, with their sons and their brethren, stood at the east end of the altar, clothed in white linen, having cymbals, stringed instruments and harps, and with them one hundred and twenty priests sounding with trumpets—indeed it came to pass, when the trumpeters and singers were as one, to make one sound to be heard in praising and thanking the Lord, and when they lifted up their voice with the trumpets and cymbals and instruments of music, and praised the Lord, saying: "For He is good, For His mercy endures forever," that the house, the house of the Lord, was filled with a cloud, so that the priests could not continue ministering because of the cloud; **for the glory of the Lord filled the house of God.***
(2 Chronicles 5:11-14, emphasis added)

ᵇ⁻ **The glory of God filled the house when the atmosphere was sanctified by thanks and praise.**

In Psalm 67:5-7 it says, "Let the people praise thee, O God; let all the people praise thee. Then shall **the earth yield her increase**; and God, even our own God, shall bless us. **God shall bless us;** and all the ends of **the earth shall fear him**" (KJV emphasis added).

The word for praise found here is an expression of thanks or praise; it is defined as a natural part of ritual or public worship, as well as personal praise to God.[2] Notice the results when praise and thanks cleanses the atmosphere: increase comes, which is a crop or wealth.

ᵇ⁻ **Praise and thanksgiving is the atmosphere that produces the increase of God, releases the blessing of God, and causes reverential fear to be known in our lives.**

Praise comes first, than the increase follows. What this means is we are thanking God before we see or possess the thing for which we are praying. King Jehoshaphat understood this principle of cleansing the atmosphere with praise and thanksgiving to invite in God's presence.

*After consulting the people, Jehoshaphat
appointed men to sing to the Lord and to
praise him for the splendor of his holiness as
they went out at the head of the army, saying:
"Give thanks to the Lord, for his love endures
forever." As they began to sing and praise,
the Lord set ambushes against the men of
Ammon and Moab and Mount Seir who were
invading Judah, and they were defeated.*
(2 Chronicles 20:21-2, NIV emphasis added)

Notice when the singers began to praise and
thank the Lord, the atmosphere was cleansed and
God sent an ambush, which is a surprise attack or an
attack from a concealed position, that shocked and
confused the enemies.

☙ Praise and thanksgiving cleansed the atmosphere and God set an ambush that confused the enemies.

God is the same yesterday, today, and forever.[3]
Our God is the God of battles, but He needs an atmosphere to do the miraculous. Jesus knew this principle when He went to raise Lazarus from the dead.

*Then they took away the stone from the place
where the dead man was lying. And Jesus
lifted up His eyes and said, "**Father, I thank
you that You have heard Me**. And I know that
You always hear Me, but because of the people
who are standing by I said this, that they may*

believe that You sent Me." Now when He had said these things, He cried with a loud voice, "Lazarus, come forth!" And he who had died came out bound hand and foot with grave clothes, and his face was wrapped with a cloth. Jesus said to them, "Loose him, and let him go." (John 11:41-44, emphasis added)

Notice before Lazarus came forth Jesus sanctified the atmosphere by thanking His Father; how profound and yet how simple.

☞ Praise and thanksgiving sanctified the atmosphere and God did the miraculous.

The Word of God is full of examples of cleansing the atmosphere through praise and thanksgiving. May the Lord illuminate this truth so that each of us would embrace this secret of the Kingdom life!

Thanksgiving Is the Highest Expression of Faith

One morning many years ago, I woke up with this thought from the Lord, "Complaining is the highest expression or manifestation of unbelief and thanksgiving is the highest expression of faith." Thanksgiving gives glory to God, as Abraham did.

He (Abraham) did not waver at the promise of God through unbelief, but was strengthened in faith, giving glory to God, and being fully convinced that what He had promised

He was also able to perform. And therefore "it was accounted to him for righteousness."
(Romans 4:20-22)

Abraham, the Father of faith, understood this principle of thanksgiving as he gave glory to God. An atmosphere of thanksgiving is to be foremost in our churches, families, marriages, and businesses today. All God asks in return for the sacrifice Jesus made at Calvary is that we be grateful and thank Him for the Cross. When the pervading or surrounding influence of a place is sanctified by thanksgiving and faith, then the Holy Spirit feels welcomed and will truly move in that place.

In Mark 6:1-6, the atmosphere of unbelief was present and Jesus could do no mighty works or miracles there. Thanksgiving creates the atmosphere for faith to abound, for love to flow, and for the joy of the Lord to be released. When God's people gather and create an atmosphere of thanksgiving, the team is encouraged and there is unity in His Body. Then the gifts of the Spirit are manifested and the supernatural power of God moves through His worshippers with signs, wonders, and miracles that bring attention, glory, and honor to His Name—not ours.

☛ **Praise and thanksgiving create an atmosphere for faith to abound.**

Let's stop right now as we finish this chapter up on atmosphere and ask ourselves if there has been any polluting of the atmosphere in our homes, churches, and marriages by our words, attitudes, actions, complaining, or murmuring. Let us repent today of hindering the move of God in our lives. May we choose to be sweet in spite of the sour situations of life that confront us! May we choose to come into His presence daily with thanksgiving and put away all whining and complaining! Once the atmosphere is clean, let's believe God for a major visitation of the Holy Spirit's power in our ministries, churches, homes, and marriages. Let's daily examine our hearts in light of gratitude and let's together release His glory in the earth. Let's seek to live in His will.

CHAPTER 2

Keys to Being in the Will of God

Some fifteen years ago I received a call from Dr. Lester Sumrall, who had impacted my life as a mentor for many years before his passing. He mentioned that he would like to meet me and Cathy for lunch with him and his wife near Ann Arbor, Michigan, about an hour outside of Windsor. We met him at the Radisson Hotel restaurant and were having lunch while enjoying gleaning from the wisdom this man of God was sharing. Then he asked me how the children were doing. I was going through a bumpy season in ministry at that time, and shared they were all doing well, but none of them were following my steps in ministry. That was the wrong answer to share with Dr. Sumrall, and he let me have it for the next half hour or so, rebuking me for my attitude, unbelief, and negativity. I was so embarrassed that my wife said my face was beet red;

I just wanted to crawl under the table and hide, go to the bathroom, or do something to get out of the line of fire that was coming at me that afternoon. After saying goodbye and embracing them, I got into the car and was feeling overwhelmed, stressed, and convicted. From that day until now, I changed my attitude, confession, and outlook about my children working with me in ministry. Our son RJ was in college taking a computer course at the time. I began praying for him, and within a few months he felt a resurgence of the call on his life to work with me in the ministry. He spent several years on the mission field in our base in the Philippines and then came home for a break and met his wife, Mary, at the church. He has served as one of my associates for the last ten years. Mary and RJ have four daughters, all living in Windsor.

I learned that as a parent we can affect the plan that God has for our children by our negativity and stinking attitude. Dr. Sumrall said that day that the greatest joy a minister can have is to see his family working together in ministry alongside one another. I realized that my complaining was blocking the plan of God for all my children in His highest and best for their lives. I recognized that there was a generational anointing and calling upon my family members in an incredible way that was to be stronger and stronger through the generations to come. The results have been amazing about what thanksgiving can do. Jake, our son-in-law, and Jaimie, our youngest daughter, are the worship leaders in our congregation, and they worship the Lord with an absolutely incredible passion and pureness. Pastor RJ is my associate, who has wisdom well beyond his years, and I just give all the deep theological questions people bring me over to him. Mellisa, my oldest daughter, runs and administrates the Open Bible Faith Fellowship office, of which I am the overseer, and she is also a master fitness trainer. She keeps all the family in good health and shape, and guides the ministry with a spirit of excellence, and is incredibly gifted in administration and organization.

My son-in-law, Shawn, who is Mellisa's husband, is one of the most talented and gifted men I know and worked as an electrician at Ford Motor Company for many years. He now runs the entire Maintenance and Grounds Department for our church, with a 130,000-square-foot facility on fifty acres. No job is too big for him and the team serving under him. Our son, Brian, who was very experienced and successful in the marketplace for the last fourteen years, has now taken over the administration of Windsor Christian Fellowship, as his degree is in human resources and his people skills are amazing. He is doing an outstanding job in building teamwork into the staff at WCF.

I am so appreciative for Dr. Sumrall's rebuke that day in the restaurant; I am so thankful to the Lord to see our children all serving God and the generational blessing flowing through to our sixteen grandchildren, at present. I believe this is the will of God for our family and am grateful for them and what God has entrusted them with as together we serve our King. The generational flow through our children is amazing. Each one is excelling in their calling, and our desire is that they go further in faith than Cathy and I have, and that our grandchildren will continue to go in the right ways of the Lord to see the transgenerational blessing continue through our bloodline.

As a leader for the last thirty-eight years in the Body of Christ, I have found one of the major requests of people in the prayer line or in counseling is to know the will of God. Many are very confused about this subject and have some pretty distorted views on what they believe the will of God is for their life.

For example, some believe the sickness in their body is God's will and their cross to carry for the rest of their lives. Yet in Scripture we see that Jesus went about doing good and healing all who were sick and oppressed of the devil.[4] If the sickness and disease was God's will, then Jesus was being awfully rebellious against His Father. We know the opposite is true because Jesus only did the things that His Father told Him to do.[5] Acts 10:38 clearly shows that God told Jesus to heal the sick and cast out devils. "How God anointed Jesus of Nazareth with the Holy Ghost and with power: who went about doing good, and healing all that were oppressed of the devil; for God was with him" (KJV).

Think about this point for just one moment. If you really believe that it is God's will for you to have some disease or sickness, then why do you go to the doctor and try to get better? That seems a bit contradictory to me. You go to the doctor because you want to get better—not worse—and it's the doctor's will to try to help you and get you feeling better.

His Word Is His Will

When I first came to Christ, I heard this statement and it has never left me: His Word is His will for my life. The word "will" is used in Scripture thousands of times, and God's will is clearly stated all throughout the Bible.

First of all, the Bible says that it is possible to know the will of God. The Apostles of the early church prayed that all believers would be filled with knowledge of God's will for their lives.

The Apostle Paul said in Colossians 1:1, "Paul, an apostle of Jesus Christ **by the will of God**, and Timothy our brother." Paul knew his apostolic calling was in the will of God. He prayed for the church in Colossians 1:9 saying, "For this cause we also, since the day we heard it, do not cease to pray for you, and to desire that ye might be **filled with the knowledge of his will** in all wisdom and spiritual understanding" (KJV). The word "filled" means to level up a hollow[6], or fill to the place of being stuffed so that you can't get another thing in you. God wants us filled with the knowledge of His will.

Then in Colossians 4:12-13 we read, "Epaphras, who is one of you, a bondservant of Christ, greets you, always laboring fervently for you in prayers, that you may stand perfect and complete in all the will of God." Epaphras was "laboring fervently," which means to struggle, to contend with adversaries, to fight, to endeavor with strenuous zeal in order to obtain something. What was it he wanted to obtain in his fervent prayers? He wanted believers to be able to "stand perfect and complete in all the will of God." Perfect means brought to its end, lacking nothing necessary to be complete, and filled up. He prayed for the saints to be lacking nothing and be filled up with the knowledge of God—the same thing Paul prayed in Chapter One.

The Bible also tells us why we need to seek to know the will of God:

> *Therefore do not be unwise, but **understand what the will of the Lord is**. And do not be drunk with wine, in which is dissipation; but be filled with the Spirit, speaking to one another in psalms and hymns and spiritual songs, singing and making melody in your heart to the Lord, giving thanks always for all things to God the Father in the name of our Lord Jesus Christ, submitting to one another in the fear of God.* (Ephesians 5:17-21).

It is very clear in Ephesians that "giving thanks always for all things to God the Father" involves understanding what the will of God is.

❧ **It is impossible for people to submit one to another if they are not grateful for the ones they are to submit to.**

The Apostle John said in 1 John 2:17, "And the world passeth away, and the lust thereof: but he that **doeth the will** of God abideth for ever" (KJV). The one that does the will of God lives forever. That is a powerful statement and reason for being in His will; it affects all eternity.

In Acts 16:20-26, we read that when we stay in the will of God nothing can come against His plan for our lives. The early church experienced severe persecution, but Paul and Silas had learned a valuable secret about staying in the will of God.

And they brought them to the magistrates, and said, "These men, being Jews, exceedingly trouble our city; and they teach customs which are not lawful for us, being Romans, to receive or observe." Then the multitude rose up together against them; and the magistrates tore off their clothes and commanded them to be beaten with rods. And when they had laid many stripes on them, they threw them into prison, commanding the jailer *to keep them securely. Having received such a charge, he put them into the inner prison and fastened their feet in the stocks. But at midnight Paul and Silas were praying and singing hymns to God, and the prisoners were listening to them. Suddenly there was a great earthquake, so that the foundations of the prison were shaken; and immediately all the doors were opened and everyone's chains were loosed.*

Paul and Silas had been beaten and locked up in the inner prison, chained with leg lock braces. The inner prison was the lowest part of the prison, where it was dark and the sewer water went through. But instead of complaining, they were praying and singing praises to God so loud that the other prisoners heard them. Suddenly, their deliverance came. Their chains and braces fell off and the prison doors were opened. That was a miracle in itself, but another great miracle happened as well. All the prisoners stayed put; no one escaped, even though their chains were off and the prison doors were open. God's will for Paul and Silas was bigger than just rescuing them from their prison.

According to Roman law, if the prisoners escaped, the jailer would have been held responsible and killed. Instead, Paul and Silas remained in the will of God, and the jailer along with his whole family were saved and baptized that very night.

Paul and Silas had learned how to stay in the will of God. Paul shares this secret with us in 1 Thessalonians 5:16-18: "Rejoice always, pray without ceasing, in everything give thanks; for this is the will of God in Christ Jesus for you." There are some really good nuggets found in these verses:

1. *We are to rejoice always. This means whether we want to or not, whether we feel like it or not, we will rejoice.*
2. *We are to pray without ceasing, or be in the attitude of prayer continually.*
3. *The third thing Paul states is that we are to be thankful in everything, in every circumstance, no matter what happens. We are to rejoice, pray continually, and give thanks no matter what because this is the will of God in Christ Jesus for you. Paul and Silas proved this is true.*

Is it possible today that many people stay locked up in their personal prison because of bitterness, strife, turmoil, unforgiveness, jealousy, and hatred? Obviously murmuring and complaining is not in the will of God, and neither is captivity.

Even in the story of Jonah, when his disobedience to the Word of God caused him to be thrown overboard, God made a way for Jonah to find his way back into God's will for his life. Jonah 1:17 says, "But God provided a great fish to swallow Jonah, and Jonah was inside the fish three days and three nights" (NIV). After three long days and nights, Jonah cried out to God from inside the fish, "'When my soul fainted within me, I remembered the Lord; and my prayer went up to You, into Your holy temple. Those who regard worthless idols forsake their own mercy. But I will sacrifice to You with the **voice of thanksgiving**; I will pay what I have vowed. Salvation is of the Lord.' So the Lord spoke to the fish, and it vomited Jonah onto dry land" (Jonah 2:7-10).

Amazingly, as soon as Jonah said, "I will sacrifice to you with the voice of thanksgiving and I will pay what I have vowed," immediately the Lord delivered him. When Jonah went to Nineveh and preached repentance to the inhabitants of the city, they believed him because they worshiped a god known as Dagon, who was half fish and half man. Many of the inhabitants of Nineveh were on the beach that day when along came a whale that emitted a man out of its mouth. The people listened to Jonah because they thought it was Dagon. Oh the wonders of God's knowledge!

What circumstance are you facing today? What trial have you been in that doesn't seem like it will ever change or end? What obstacles are you facing at this very moment? Whatever it might be, the Word of God says give thanks and your deliverance will come. Somebody reading this right now is in a life and death challenge and God says to you, "Bring that sacrifice of thanks now and the shift will take place." Somebody else reading this book is in a prison of despair and you have been there a long time. God is saying to you:

☛ **If you will stop and begin to praise and thank the Lord, that grief will lift and joy will return to your life right this moment.**

There is someone who was betrayed by a spouse and your life has virtually stopped. You're like a spiritual zombie, but when you lift up your voice with thanksgiving to your God and Deliverer, the shackles will break off your mind and the tormentors will be out of a job. Now you can understand why thanksgiving is so important to being in the center of the will of God for your lives.

Do Not Quench the Spirit

The Apostle Paul told us to rejoice, continually pray, and give thanks to God in all circumstances because this was God's will for us. Then he follows this list with another list which starts in 1 Thessalonians 5:19 and says, "Do not **quench** the Spirit." *Quench* means to extinguish, to put out, to suppress, or stifle divine influence. It also means to restrain, hinder, or smother the operation of, in this case, the Holy Spirit. As a former asthmatic, I know what it is like to try to get your breath when something is hindering or smothering your ability to breathe. You're wheezing and gasping to try to get air into your lungs. This is the description Paul uses to explain what happens when a believer rejects gratefulness; he quenches the Spirit.

When I saw this many years ago, I quickly realized that the Holy Spirit wanted to move in my life but I had quenched Him by my attitude of complaining and grumbling. Every time a believer complains instead of being thankful, they literally block their own deliverance. Negativity, criticalness, and murmuring quench the Spirit, hindering Him from moving in our lives. But the sacrifice of thanksgiving keeps us under an open Heaven so the angels can work for us who are heirs of salvation.

☙ God will arise and scatter His enemies who are attacking our lives; He will lift us above our circumstances.

What a powerful revelation that ungrateful language has the ability to stop the anointing from flowing out of us, suffocate the spirit man inside, and extinguish the fire in our hearts for things of God. Our complaining and grumbling can stifle the move of the Spirit and suppress or hold down the flow of God in our lives. The Word teaches us that complaining, murmuring, and grumbling drives the Spirit away from us but grateful, appreciative, and thankful language invites the Holy Spirit to become active in our lives.

Can you remember being in a room having a pleasant conversation and enjoying all the sharing until one negative, unthankful complainer comes into the room and starts grumbling? Almost instantaneously the atmosphere becomes depressing, heavy, and negative emotions begin to surface. Most of us would want to get out of there and away from the negativity. It's the same type of situation in the spirit realm. All the power of Heaven that is available to us is stifled and the Holy Spirit and God's angels are forced out of such an atmosphere.

Another example is someone lights up a cigarette in the room and you're a nonsmoker. All of a sudden your eyes are burning, your breathing is hindered, and the room becomes clouded. You want to get out of there as fast as you can. That is the same way it is with the spirit realm. No warring angel wants to hang around doubt, discouragement, negativity, and complaining.

God can turn every situation around that life may bring if the atmosphere is clear for Him to move in. Problems can be quickly solved and the impossible can become possible with God. Failures in life can be quickly turned into stepping-stones to move us up to the next level in God. Where there is confusion and strife, thanksgiving can bring peace, soundness of mind, and clarity of purpose almost immediately. I have learned that if I keep an attitude of gratitude, contradictions of vision, direction, and purpose will quickly fade away and I can stay secure in the will of God.

I learned this principle very early in my Christian walk of faith. I had a great job, great pay, and was working a secular job in the produce industry. Just after graduating from Bible school in late May of 1982, I moved from Broken Arrow, Oklahoma, back to Detroit, Michigan, and took a job with my former employer, The Aunt Mid Produce Company. I was working a lot of hours and making good money. Then in August things started slowing down and because I was low man on the seniority list, I was laid off first. I was just short of having my three months in that job and that would have made me eligible to collect unemployment. I had a wife and three children at the time, house payments, and no money in savings. I was barely making ends meet even with this job.

When my boss came and broke the news at 5:00 a.m. on a Friday morning, he was very sad. To the shock of my employer, I immediately responded with thanksgiving. I told him I appreciated all that he had done for me in hiring me back after Bible school and I was persuaded that God had something good in store for me just around the corner. He walked away from me a bit troubled, not understanding completely why or how I had responded to him with such joy.

On the following Sunday morning at 8:00 a.m., I received a call from a leader of a prayer meeting that I had spoken at in Windsor, Ontario, just a few weeks prior to this layoff. The man's name was Nello Paolini, and he asked me if I would consider being the pastor of this small group of people in Windsor. He said they could pay me two hundred dollars Canadian a week. In the natural, it didn't look like the most promising offer or future, but I said, "Yes." That was the beginning of Windsor Christian Fellowship, where I have been the senior pastor for over twenty years. I believe my attitude of thanksgiving opened the atmosphere up for God to make provision and direct my path. I know without any doubt that pastoring WCF is the center of the will of God for my life. The people are amazing, dedicated, and committed to the cause of Christ. They are passionate to see loved ones come into His Kingdom, and it is an honor to serve them as their pastor along with my wife Cathy.

I wonder how many men and women are frustrated, stressed out, depressed, and miserable because they complain and abort their future by being ungrateful for what they have. Grumblers very seldom have good things happen to them in life. They live a boring, unproductive life. But those who show themselves thankful for what they have been given live an exciting, enthusiastic, and fulfilling life. God's blessings continually flow towards them as they journey through life. I am totally persuaded that God wants me to have life more abundantly or life that increases and gives meaning, fulfillment, and satisfaction.

☞ **An *attitude of gratitude* keeps His blessings flowing in and through my life.**

God wants you to have an abundant life with blessings overflowing. Jesus said in John 10:10, "The thief cometh not, but for to steal, and to kill, and to destroy: I am come that they might have life, and that they might have it more abundantly" (KJV).

Manifestations of Quenching the Spirit

Take a moment and review this list of ways you may be quenching the Spirit in your life and keeping God's blessing from freely flowing through your life. If you recognize that you are doing any of them, use the solution offered after each one to stop this destructive behavior.

#1- Counting your troubles and not your blessings?

Solution: Whatsoever things are good, true, lovely, and of a good report, my brethren, think on these things. (See Philippians 4:8)

#2- Worrying every day about something?

Solution: Thanksgiving helps you enjoy life and those around you. (See 1 Thessalonians 5:18)

#3- Feeling sorry for yourself, and having pity parties?

Solution: Woe is me is a mindset. Never base your life on your present circumstances, but on God's promise to you. (See Romans 8:31)

#4- Trying to compare and compete with others?

Solution: The power twins of hell are comparing and competition among us. Refuse to allow them to take up residence in your life. (See Galatians 6:4-5)

#5- Insisting upon your rights and your way?

Solution: Seek to do things God's way and He promises He will provide for all of your needs. (See Matthew 6:33)

#6- Complaining about things you can't change in the natural anyway?

Solution: Always look for the bright side of life. You may not be able to change some things, but you can always change your attitude and your confession of faith to a positive one. I have learned over many years to keep a simple motto before my eyes in the midst of life's challenges: "Stay sweet, Rick, in spite of the sour situation." When I consciously make that choice I am never disappointed. (See Romans 5:1-5)

As we close this chapter, if you realize today that you have been quenching God's Spirit by ungratefulness in your life, then stop for a moment and acknowledge this sin to God and ask for His help to overcome the negativity and criticalness in your life. Now you're a recipient of His supernatural peace, power, and provision to flood your heart and mind.

Now imagine that you can release God's glory in the earth. Next you will read on to discover the secret to releasing heavenly glory!

CHAPTER 3

Keys to Releasing God's Glory in the Earth

Jesus gave the glory that He had to the church so that they may be one. I recognized that part of God's end-time plan was for His Body to be one. I remember almost twenty-nine years ago when I had just started WCF and we were in a rented facility called the Teutonia Club in Windsor. I had personally invited all the ministers in the city to join me for a time of prayer at the Teutonia Club to specifically pray for our city and the Body of Christ working together. Amazingly after all the preparations, renting the hall, coffeepots, donuts, etc., no one showed up but a few leaders from our church. I was discouraged but felt that this was something the Lord was leading me into, and to keep serving in faith and leave the results up to God.

Over many years we have seen ministers come together to pray, fellowship, and strategize on how to be a greater witness in the city for Christ. Once we started to connect, the direct result was barriers, walls, and misunderstandings between churches and ministers were obliterated by His Grace, and His Glory could now be released. We recognize that in the essentials we must have oneness, in the nonessentials we must have liberty, but in all things we must have love among us. Today in the city of Windsor, churches sow into other churches and the outreaches they are doing in our community serve the less fortunate and help build strong families and marriages. We celebrate diversity and have come to recognize that we are not in a competition with one another, but are there to help complete one another as we work together.

Some of my closest friends in ministry today are pastors in churches in Essex County who truly love our community and practice the principle of preferring one another more highly than themselves. This has truly been a delight to our Heavenly Father and has opened up the heavens around us for His greater Glory to be released. I believe when ministers truly love one another that the entire region and heavens over them open up and His Glory now can be released upon them. What I learned over these many years of serving in my community is that through faith and patience, we inherit the promises of God. We truly need one another, and must work as a unified team so that His Glory can flow through us in our homes, marriages, families, churches, and ministries that the Lord has entrusted to us.

Jesus lived and practiced a life of gratitude before His Father. He never murmured in spite of a critical and judgmental group of religious leaders around Him. He never yielded to the works of darkness that attacked Him. He never stopped showing the Father's character, love, heart, forgiveness, justice, and mercy to all He came in contact with. Thanksgiving is the key to releasing God's glory in the earth today.

We have already read about Solomon dedicating the Temple in 2 Chronicles 5. At that moment, the glory of God came in so that the priests could not stand and minister. They had an all-out worship service and the presence of God was experienced among them. In this chapter, I want to share that the glory is not coming down like in the Old Covenant but is already inside of us. This revelation has changed the way I pray and communicate with the Holy Spirit.

☞ Acknowledging *we already have it* releases God's glory in the earth.

His divine power has given us everything we need for life and godliness through our knowledge of him who called us by his own glory and goodness. Through these he has given us his very great and precious promises, so that through them you may participate in the divine nature and escape the corruption in the world caused by evil desires. (2 Peter 1:3-4 NIV)

The first key to releasing God's glory in the earth is to realize "we already have it." If we are praying for something we already have we will become quite frustrated. These four words have changed the way I look at prayer. **"We already have it."** God has already deposited into us everything we need to participate in His divine nature. His laws are in our hearts along with grace, ability, love, longsuffering, patience, goodness, kindness, humility, righteousness, forgiveness, joy, peace, faithfulness, self-control, gentleness, compassion, mercy, gifting, talents, and faith.

"For it is God who commanded light to shine out of darkness, who has shone in our hearts to give the light of the knowledge of the glory of God in the face of Jesus Christ. But we have this **treasure** in earthen vessels that the excellence of the power may be of God and not of us" (2 Corinthians 4:6-7). The word "treasure" means a deposit, the place in which goods and precious things are collected and laid up. The treasure, the glory of God has been deposited inside us, earthen vessels.

☞ Unity in His Body, the Church, manifests God's glory in the earth.

In John 17:22 Jesus said in His prayer for all believers, "And the glory which You gave Me I have given them, that they may be one just as We are one." Jesus taught us that the reason the glory was given was so that we may be one united body with Christ as the head. The devil is a master at sowing division into the Body of Christ. He realizes by division he can hinder, thwart, and disrupt the Kingdom of God in the earth. Look at all the divisions, church splits, and mean-spirited people that have caused great havoc and hindered the spreading of the Gospel in our world. Where there is unity in the Body of Christ, the glory is manifested and people are drawn to Christ. Where there is disunity, the advancement of the Gospel is greatly hindered.

☛ Thankfulness in the midst of trials and suffering releases God's glory in the earth.

Right after Paul shares the revelation that we have this treasure in our earthen vessels, he explains how to handle trials and suffering so as to see God's glory abound in the earth.

But we have this treasure in earthen vessels, that the excellence of the power may be of God and not of us. We are hard-pressed on every side, yet not crushed; we are perplexed, but not in despair; persecuted, but not forsaken; struck down, but not destroyed—always carrying about in the body the dying of the Lord Jesus, that the life of Jesus also may be manifested in our body. For we who live are always delivered to death for Jesus' sake, that the life of Jesus also may be manifested in our mortal flesh. So then death is working in us, but life in you. And since we have the same spirit of faith, according to what is written, "I believed and therefore I spoke," we also

believe and therefore speak, knowing that He
who raised up the Lord Jesus will also raise
us up with Jesus, and will present us with you.
For all things are for your sakes, that grace,
*having spread through the many, **may cause***
thanksgiving to abound to the glory of God.
(2 Corinthians 4:7-15, emphasis added)

Look at the hardships Paul spoke about that
follow the glory. The purpose of the glory is to manifest the life of Jesus and that comes through rec-
ognizing our sufficiency is Him and not ourselves
as we go through hardships. In 1 Peter you will see
the words "suffer" and "suffering" sixteen times.
You will also see the words "glory," "glorying," and
"glorified" sixteen times, which tells us that suffering is the pathway to release the glory of God in us.

But there is one more point that is essential for
the glory to be released and that is also revealed
in 2 Corinthians 4:13-15, "And since we have the
same spirit of faith, according to what is written, **'I**
believed and therefore I spoke,' we also believe
and therefore speak, knowing that He who raised up
the Lord Jesus will also raise us up with Jesus, and
will present us with you. For all things are for your
sakes, that grace, having spread through the many,
may **cause thanksgiving to abound to the glory of**
God." Once again we see that when thanksgiving is
inside of us, words of gratitude are coming out of
us causing the glory of God to abound on the earth.
Abound means to occur or exist in great quantities.

When thanksgiving comes out of our hearts in the midst of adversity, hardships, and suffering for the Gospel, the Holy Spirit will move mightily, displaying the power that is on the inside of us, and others will see the glory of God manifested. God can take the toughest tests of life and turn them into a powerful testimony of His love. It is where He can take the greatest trials of our faith and turn them into tremendous victories. God can even take the messes we get ourselves into and turn them into a message for His glory.

☞ Acknowledging God as your answer releases His glory in the earth.

There are many examples in Scripture of what appears to the world as a negative past being suddenly turned into a bright fulfilling future as God's glory is manifested in the lives of those who chose to remain in an attitude of gratitude.

Even when the intimidation of hell threatened to stifle God's purpose in Peter after he denied the Lord Jesus three times, Peter preached with a new boldness that drew thousands to Jesus as God's glory manifested on the earth.

This is where the shame you've lived with is turned around, like Rahab the Harlot's shame is turned into fame in the Hall of Fame chapter of Hebrews 11. Your sorrow is turned into laughter and your fear is turned into great faith like in the lives of Abraham and Sarah. This is where your insecurity of the past becomes the stepping-stone of great confidence in your future, and finally where your hurt and pain are turned into health and wholeness. Every one of these things are possible if you lift up your voice to thank God and acknowledge Him as your Deliverer, your Healer, your Provider, your Shield, your Rock, your Fortress, and your Mighty Warrior in Zion.

How many times in the midst of the storms of life do we complain and even question why all this is happening, rather than speaking His promises and releasing the Glory of God into those circumstances? Next time the enemy brings an accusation, condemnation, or assault against your mind, just stop for one moment and begin to praise our King. Thank Him for what He has done for you in the past and thank Him that He is on the scene to turn things around. Remember the glory was given so that we may be one in Him and that His power and love may be revealed through His Body.

Where can you turn to thank Him in all things? There is a place in Scripture filled with thanksgiving and I want to take you there now.

CHAPTER 4

Thanksgiving in Psalms

In June of 1998, at the age of fifty-one, Marilyn, one of my parishioners, went through the "valley of weeping." She will tell you that it was not a place of refreshing springs. She had been experiencing occasional neck pain throughout the spring months, but awoke one early June morning with extreme pain and nausea. She was told by her doctor that it was probably just a pulled muscle and that it would improve with rest. The pain continued to increase over the next few weeks, and Marilyn spent most of her days either in bed or in the hospital emergency room. There didn't seem to be any medication that lessened the pain. Marilyn lost twenty-eight pounds because she couldn't eat. She says her days blurred one into another, but the nights were unbearable. It was on one of those frighteningly lonely nights that Marilyn decided to forego her usual Bible reading and focus on the book of Psalms. She kept a journal of all the verses that gave her hope and believed that

Psalm 84 was something God wanted her to know. She read:

*What joy for those whose strength comes
    from the Lord,
    who have set their minds on a pilgrimage
    to Jerusalem.
When they walk through the Valley of Weeping,
    it will become a place of refreshing
    springs.
The autumn rains will clothe it with
    blessings.
They will continue to grow stronger,
    and each of them will appear before God
    in Jerusalem.*

(Psalm 84:5-7 NLT)

Marilyn learned that God was showing her that He would make her happy on her life's journey (a pilgrimage to Jerusalem) as she sought to know Him and live for him. God could make the valley of weeping a place of refreshing springs where pools of blessing collect and strength returns. Her focus changed from asking God for healing and crying out in pain to thanksgiving and praise. She became determined to thank Him for her life, her family, and her salvation.

There is a resolve that comes when there is nothing you can do except trust God. She says that she remembers feeling like she just took a deep breath and rested in God's arms. Her life was in His hands and she knew He had her best interests at heart.

On Wednesday, July 29, Marilyn decided to go to the evening service at church for prayer. Following the service she went to the hospital emergency room again and after waiting eight hours, she saw a doctor who called in a neurologist who was on duty. He recommended she get an MRI immediately and then go home and wait for the results. Marilyn got a call early Thursday morning asking her to go see a neurosurgeon at the hospital. She told her that her C6-C7 disc had completely disintegrated and that she needed emergency surgery. This neurosurgeon made arrangements for the surgery on Friday even though the hospital operating rooms were on a week of vacation. Marilyn was admitted on Thursday evening and had successful surgery on Friday morning.

She was told several times that it was a miracle that they opened the operating rooms for the surgery and that the doctors and nurses were available on such short notice. Marilyn agrees. It was a miracle. She knows that God orchestrated the chance meeting with the neurologist in the ER and the brave neurosurgeon who challenged the hospital staff to help when it was inconvenient.

ᴥ God brings springs of blessings when we decide to thank Him and put our trust in Him.

Psalms grew out of the life of a community of faith as the people used their songs and poetry to worship God. David is traditionally seen as the author of most of the Psalms, as well as Asaph, who wrote Psalms 73-83, and Korah, who wrote Psalms

42, 44-49, 84-85, and 87-88. Many Jewish people today read through the Book of Psalms on a weekly or monthly basis because it is viewed in Jewish tradition as a vehicle for gaining God's favor. Psalms are often quoted in times of adversity, distress, and challenges. Psalms are recited after services for the security and peace of the State of Israel. The Psalms are some of the most widely read portions of the Old Testament today and are quoted extensively by the early church fathers as well as throughout church history. They have been the basis of much of the hymnody and choruses of the church.

In both ancient Israel and today's world, poetry and music are the means by which people expressed the deepest of human feelings and emotions; the most profound of insights and revelations; the most tragic and joyous of human experiences. Jesus and the writers of the New Testament used 116 references from Psalms. They were a vital part of the early church and should be for us today as well.

Speak and Sing the Psalms

There are three common New Testament admonishments to sing and speak psalms.

- **Ephesians 5:17-21** instructs, "Therefore do not be unwise, but understand what the will of the Lord is. And do not be drunk with wine, in which is dissipation; but be filled with the Spirit, **speaking to one another in psalms and hymns and spiritual songs,** singing and making melody in your heart to the Lord, giving thanks always for all things to God the Father in the name of our Lord Jesus Christ, submitting to one another in the fear of God."

- **Colossians 3:12-17** exhorts, "Therefore, as the elect of God, holy and beloved, put on tender mercies, kindness, humility, meekness, longsuffering; bearing with one another, and forgiving one another, if anyone has a complaint against another; even as Christ forgave you, so you also must do. But above all these things put on love, which is the bond of perfection. And let the peace of God rule in your hearts, to which also you were called in **one body; and be thankful.** Let the word of Christ dwell in you richly in all wisdom, **teaching and admonishing one another in psalms and hymns and spiritual songs**, singing with grace in your hearts to the Lord. And whatever you do in word or deed, do all in the name of the Lord Jesus, **giving thanks** to God the Father through Him."

- **James 5:13** teaches, "Is anyone among you suffering? Let him pray. Is anyone cheerful? Let him sing psalms."

Notice in each one of these passages there is an admonishment to thanksgiving or a warning against grumbling, which is the opposite of thanksgiving, as in James.

Promises from the Psalms

One of my favorites for standing on the promises of God is Psalm 34:4-10, "I sought the Lord, and He heard me, and delivered me from all my fears. They looked to Him and were radiant, and their faces were not ashamed. This poor man cried out, and the Lord heard him, and saved him out of all his troubles. The angel of the Lord encamps all around those who fear Him, and delivers them. Oh, taste and see that the Lord is good; blessed is the man who trusts in Him! Oh, fear the Lord, you His saints! There is no want to those who fear Him. The young lions lack and suffer hunger; But those who seek the Lord shall not lack any good thing."

Also verses 17-19, "The righteous cry out, and the Lord hears, and delivers them out of all their troubles. The Lord is near to those who have a broken heart, and saves such as have a contrite spirit. Many are the afflictions of the righteous; but the Lord delivers him out of them all."

We read all these amazing promises in the Psalms, yet I personally know many who have stood on these promises and never had their promises come to pass in their life. This greatly troubled me for many years until the revelation came as to *why* the promises were not fulfilled for them. I don't feel I need to have answers for everything that happens in a person's life, but some reasons do seem to me to appear obvious and worthy of explaining.

I want you to note that the promises I stated in Psalm 34 began with verse four. This seems to be a pattern throughout the Psalms when it comes to the promises of God. As I discovered this pattern, it tells me there are at least three verses of conditions given that have to be fulfilled for the promises listed in that Psalm to manifest. Many Christians become very disillusioned and offended with the things of God today if they claim the promise with sincere faith and it does not happen. They blame God when in fact God is not the problem. Their lack of understanding concerning the process may be the reason the promise has not been fulfilled. If they have not heeded the warnings, or followed the instructions listed before the promise, God cannot answer their prayers. God is consistent and faithful; He must hold to whatever He has said in His Word.

Many Christians are not aware that there are 1,209 times where the word "because" is used in the Scriptures. *Because* means for the reason that or since. There are also 220 uses of the word "cause," which means that which produces a result or effect, the origin or motive of an action. The word "if" is used 1,637 times. *If* means on the condition or supposition that. The word "then," meaning immediately afterwards or for this reason, is used 3,978 times. The sum total for the use of those four words is that there are over 7,000 specific reasons why promises work for some and will not work for others. It also confirms that taking Scriptures out of context can in fact cause us to fail to meet the conditions listed for that promise to be fulfilled.

My point for sharing this with you is that in Psalm 34:1-3, we find the foundation for the promises listed in verses 4-10. They are the conditions that need to be met before the promise comes to pass.

Psalm 34:1-3 says, "I will bless the Lord at all times; His praise shall continually be in my mouth. My soul shall make its boast in the Lord; the humble shall hear of it and be glad. Oh, magnify the Lord with me, and let us exalt His name together."

Notice David begins with, "I will bless the Lord at all times; His praise shall continually be in my mouth." There are three powerful observations I discovered from this beginning verse.

> *#1- Our will is involved in this, not our feelings or emotions.*
> *#2- We are to bless or thank the Lord at all times, in all seasons of our lives.*
> *#3- His praise or celebration is on our lips continually, without ceasing, which means it has become a habit. When we have something deep inside our heart it becomes as natural to us as breathing.*

Next it says, "My soul shall make its boast in the Lord."

☛ **It is the humble and thankful—not the arrogant, prideful, selfish, self-centered person—but the humble or teachable one who will receive the promises of God.**

"Oh, magnify the Lord with me, and let us exalt His name together." The focus is on Him, not us. We are to magnify the Lord and exalt His name. And we are to do this together. With whom are we to join together to praise God? When the people of God come together in unity to celebrate His goodness, are grateful through all the seasons of life, walking in humility of spirit, and focusing on Him, then verse four states, "I sought the Lord, and He heard me, And delivered me from all my fears."

☛ **Without thanksgiving at all times, in all seasons and as a way of life, the promises of God won't be activated in our lives.**

To receive the promise of deliverance in the day of trouble that is given at the end of Psalm 50:15, we must follow the instructions given in Psalm 50:14 and the beginning of verse 15. "Offer to God thanksgiving, and pay your vows to the Most High. Call upon Me in the day of trouble; I will deliver you, and you shall glorify Me."

The Sacrifice of Praise and Thanksgiving

Psalm 116:16-17 says, "I will offer to You the sacrifice of thanksgiving, And will call upon the name of the Lord." At times, thanksgiving involves sacrifice. We may not feel like thanking God in the midst of the storm or praising Him when we are in the midst of tribulation. But when we remember His goodness revealed to each of us at the Cross, we can't help but praise and thank Him. Once we thank and praise Him, then we can call on His Name to move on our behalf, not before.

Psalm 95:1-2 invites, "Oh come, let us sing to the Lord! Let us shout joyfully to the Rock of our salvation. Let us come before His presence with thanksgiving; Let us shout joyfully to Him with psalms."

Psalm 100:4-5 instructs us to, "Enter into His gates with thanksgiving, And into His courts with praise. Be thankful to Him, and bless His name. For the Lord is good; His mercy is everlasting, And His truth endures to all generations."

These two psalms both make reference to our attitude as we come before Him. We must come with thanksgiving, not complaining and angry, then we can unburden our hearts to our Heavenly Father.

☛ **When we remember His goodness revealed to each of us at the Cross, we can't help but praise and thank Him. Once we thank and praise Him, then we can call on His Name to move on our behalf, not before.**

Consider these verses on thanksgiving from the Psalms:

"Oh, that men would give thanks to the Lord for His goodness, and for His wonderful works to the children of men! Let them sacrifice the sacrifices of thanksgiving, and declare His works with rejoicing" (Psalm 107:21-22).

"I will offer to You the sacrifice of thanksgiving, And will call upon the name of the Lord" (Psalm 116:16-17).

The Book of Psalms is so rich, with a theme of gratitude flowing through them. May we read them with appreciation and see His promises released in our lives. As we finish this chapter, it's a good time to examine our hearts to see if there is anything inside of us that we are holding against anyone. Is there any promise that we stood on that never came to pass that has left us inwardly angry, frustrated, and disappointed with God? Have we slipped into the daily habit of coming before the Lord with a list of complaints, frustrations, and hurts rather than with thanks and praise?

Why not learn from the writers of the psalms and start your day by proclaiming "with the voice of thanksgiving, and tell of all (God's) wondrous works" (Psalm 26:7). Now let's turn to praying with thanksgiving.

CHAPTER 5

Thanksgiving in Prayer

I pray on a daily basis for each of my married children and their spouses, as well as for our sixteen grandchildren. But every prayer is one of thanks for them. I thank the Lord that their desires are His desires. I thank Him that their decisions are the right decisions. I express my thanksgiving to God that their passion and love for God is increasing daily. I thank Him that they have a hedge of protection around them and that the evil one cannot touch them. I thank Him that daily they will seek Him and come before Him. I thank God that harmony is prevailing in their homes, and that all their children will be walking in the example of their parents in the fear of the Lord. Every request I make for Cathy and my marriage is with thanksgiving. Every prayer for the church is with thanksgiving. It has now become a habit to see our future through the eyes of thanksgiving. In other words, thanksgiving is prophetic.

☛ **We pray into our future; we deposit the substance of our faith into the hands of Christ, who shapes the future we pray for in His will and in the Spirit.**

Prayer is essential for a healthy walk with the Lord, yet so many believers struggle in this area. I pray this chapter will help you cultivate a great prayer life with the Lord and His Spirit. One of the greatest examples in the Bible of someone with a consistent, steady, uncompromising prayer life is Daniel. We see two references in Scripture of his prayer life. The first was when he and the three Hebrew children were about to be killed by the king if they could not interpret his dream, and the second was a major betrayal by jealous coworkers who set Daniel up.

Notice Daniel's praise, thanks, and acknowledgement of God in his life in Daniel 2:20-23:

*"Blessed be the name of God forever and ever, for wisdom and might are His. And He changes the times and the seasons; He removes kings and raises up kings; He gives wisdom to the wise and knowledge to those who have understanding. He reveals deep and secret things; He knows what is in the darkness, and light dwells with Him. **I thank You and praise You, O God of my fathers;** You have given me wisdom and might, and have now made known to me what we asked of You, For You have made known to us the king's demand."*

Notice before the betrayal and ultimate trip in the lion's den came a quality decision from Daniel to keep the habit of praying with thanksgiving in Daniel 6:1-10:

It pleased Darius to set over the kingdom one hundred and twenty satraps, to be over the whole kingdom; and over these, three governors, of whom Daniel was one, that the satraps might give account to them, so that the king would suffer no loss. Then this Daniel distinguished himself above the governors and satraps, because an excellent spirit was in him; and the king gave thought to setting him over the whole realm. So the governors and satraps sought to find some charge against Daniel concerning the kingdom; but they could find no charge or fault, because he was faithful; nor was there any error or fault found in him. Then these men said, "We shall not find any charge against this Daniel unless we find it against him concerning the law of his God." So these governors and satraps thronged before the king, and said thus to him: "King Darius, live forever! All the governors of the kingdom, the administrators and satraps, the counselors and advisors, have consulted together to establish a royal statute and to make a firm decree, that whoever petitions any god or man for thirty days, except you, O king, shall be cast into the den of lions. Now, O king, establish the decree and sign the writing, so that it cannot be changed, according to the law of the Medes and Persians, which does not alter." Therefore King Darius signed the written decree. **Now when Daniel knew that the writing was signed, he went home. And in his upper room, with his windows open toward Jerusalem, he knelt down on his knees three times that day, and prayed and gave thanks** *before his God, as was his custom since early days.*

When Daniel was thrown into the lion's den, the atmosphere was filled with the glory of God and the lions could not harm him. Thanksgiving sanctified the atmosphere for Daniel to be protected and preserved.

I ask myself, "How many have pulled the hedge of protection down because of grumbling and complaining all day long about every trivial situation that comes their way?"

I also wonder how our lives would be changed if when we were betrayed we turned our face towards the Lord and gave thanks, knowing that He is listening and is willing to intervene when the atmosphere is cleansed. Daniel had an amazing commitment to come before the Lord three times a day with thanks and prayer.

In the New Testament, the apostle Paul must have picked up on this as he writes Philippians 4:6-7: "Be anxious for nothing, but in everything by prayer and supplication, **with thanksgiving,** let your requests be made known to God; and the peace of God, which surpasses all understanding, will guard your hearts and minds through Christ Jesus."

So many bring their specific requests before the Lord day after day, but it's more of a complaint list than anything else. When we thank in advance before the prayer or supplication is made, we connect with the living God by faith. This is how things work in the spirit world as Abraham taught us; God calls the things that be not as though they were (see Romans 4:17-18). Thanksgiving is an acknowledgement to God that you have trusted Him in the past and you are entrusting to Him your future, your prayers, and your circumstances.

Thanksgiving Is the Highest Expression of Faith

It might surprise you to know that Jesus did not ordinarily pray for miracles. At times, He simply gave thanks. We see a powerful illustration of the relationship between prayer and thanksgiving in John 6:4-14, in the account of the multiplication of the loaves and fish.

Now the Passover, a feast of the Jews, was near. Then Jesus lifted up His eyes, and seeing a great multitude coming toward Him, He said to Philip, "Where shall we buy bread, that these may eat?" But this He said to test him, for He Himself knew what He would do. Philip answered Him, "Two hundred denarii worth of bread is not sufficient for them, that *every one of them may have a little." One of His disciples, Andrew, Simon Peter's brother, said to Him, "There is a lad here who has five barley loaves and two small fish, but what are they among so many?" Then Jesus said, "Make the people sit down." Now there was much grass in the place. So the men sat down, in number about five thousand. **And Jesus took the loaves, and when He had given thanks He distributed them to the disciples**, and the disciples to those sitting down; and likewise of the fish, as much as they wanted. So when they were filled, He said to His disciples, "Gather up the fragments that remain, so that nothing is lost." Therefore they gathered them up, and filled twelve baskets with the fragments of the five barley loaves which were left over by those who had eaten. Then those men, when they had seen the sign that Jesus did, said, "This is truly the Prophet who is to come into the world."*

Jesus took the loaves and the fish, gave thanks, and offered them to the disciples to distribute among the people. By this simple act, the bread and fish were multiplied. Thanksgiving is the highest expression of faith. God knew the need before it existed. Consequently, Jesus didn't pray that God would meet the need. By faith He simply gave thanks for the provision and proceeded to feed the multitude!

☙ **Too often prayers are mixed with unbelief; but thanksgiving, before seeing the answer, is the highest manifestation or expression of faith.**

The Prayers of Paul

The apostle Paul prayed for the churches that he established and ministered to. These prayers can be prayed for our churches and families today as well.

Paul's prayer for the Philippians reads, "*Paul and Timothy, bondservants of Jesus Christ, To all the saints in Christ Jesus who are in Philippi, with the bishops and deacons: Grace to you and peace from God our Father and the Lord Jesus Christ. I thank my God upon every remembrance of you, always in every prayer of mine making request for you all with joy, for your fellowship in the gospel from the first day until now, being confident of this very thing, that He who has begun a good work in you will complete it until the day of Jesus Christ*" (Philippians 1:1-6).

Paul's prayer for the Ephesians declares, "*Therefore I also, after I heard of your faith in the Lord Jesus and your love for all the saints, do not cease to give thanks for you, making mention of you in my prayers: that the God of our Lord Jesus Christ, the Father of glory, may give to you the spirit of wisdom and revelation in the knowledge of Him, the eyes of your understanding being enlightened; that you may know what is the hope of His calling, what are the riches of the glory of His inheritance in the saints, and what is the exceeding greatness of His power toward us who believe, according to the working of His mighty power which He worked in Christ when He raised Him from the dead and seated Him at His right hand in the heavenly places, far above all principality and power and might and dominion, and every name that is named, not only in this age but also in that which is to come"* (Ephesians 1:15-21).

Paul's prayer for the Colossians intercedes, "Paul, an apostle of Jesus Christ by the will of God, and Timothy our brother, To the saints and faithful brethren in Christ who are in Colosse: Grace to you and peace from God our Father and the Lord Jesus Christ. ***We give thanks to the God and Father of our Lord Jesus Christ, praying always for you,*** *since we heard of your faith in Christ Jesus and of your love for all the saints; because of the hope which is laid up for you in heaven, of which you heard before in the word of the truth of the gospel, which has come to you, as it has also in all the world, and is bringing forth fruit, as it is also among you since the day you heard and knew the grace of God in truth; as you also learned from Epaphras, our dear fellow servant, who is a faithful minister of Christ on your behalf, who also declared to us your love in the Spirit"* (Colossians 1:1-8 emphasis added).

Notice the common denominator in all of Paul's prayers for the churches was that of appreciation, gratitude, and thanksgiving. I have learned that when people feel valued, appreciated, and are thanked from a sincere heart they will become your most loyal, committed, faithful, and dedicated people in the church.

Even when Paul had to strongly correct and rebuke the Corinthian leaders, he started off his letter with thanksgiving: "To the church of God which is at Corinth, to those who are sanctified in Christ Jesus, called to be saints, with all who in every place call on the name of Jesus Christ our Lord, both theirs and ours: Grace to you and peace from God our Father and the Lord Jesus Christ. **I thank my God always concerning you** for the grace of God which was given to you by Christ Jesus" (1 Corinthians 1:2-4 emphasis added).

Paul had some strong correction for divisions, competition, incestuous relationships in the church, drunkenness at communion, taking one another to court, meats sacrificed to idols, misuse of spiritual gifts, and misunderstandings on the doctrine of resurrections. Yet the Corinthians knew he appreciated them and valued them. If a person does not appreciate the people he is correcting and is not thankful for them, then the way he corrects them will usually be with harshness, anger, and belittling, which is the opposite of the way that Paul handled correction.

Finally, let's read a Scripture on prayer with thanksgiving that is found in 1 Timothy 1:18-2:4.

This charge I commit to you, son Timothy, according to the prophecies previously made concerning you, that by them you may wage the good warfare, having faith and a good conscience, which some having rejected, concerning the faith have suffered shipwreck, of whom are Hymenaeus and Alexander, whom

I delivered to Satan that they may learn not to blaspheme. Therefore I exhort first of all that supplications, prayers, intercessions, and giving of thanks be made for all men, for kings and all who are in authority, that we may lead a quiet and peaceable life in all godliness and reverence. For this is good and acceptable in the sight of God our Savior, who desires all men to be saved and to come to the knowledge of the truth.

The context of this chapter comes after the two ministers, Hymenaeus and Alexander, made a shipwreck of their faith. Paul puts a "therefore" because of these two men, who were leaders in the early church, getting off track. Paul says first of all that supplications, prayers, intercessions, and giving of thanks be made for all men, for kings, and all who are in authority. The "all men" would be those ministers and leaders in the church world, as well as kings of nations and all those who are in authority, for they will have influence in their area.

Let's talk for a moment about ministers of the Gospel who get off track. First of all, what is our response to be? Our response is to lift prayers up for them to God in intercession with thanksgiving. God's plan and desire is that the individuals who got off track would get back on track. Oftentimes all we can see is the hurt, abuse, and pain they have caused people in their churches and in the Body of Christ. Yet, we can never forget that God still loves them and desires them to turn from their sin and rebellion and get back on track. Thanksgiving provides the means for them to turn around as they realize you and I really do care for them and we are grateful for the lives that they have touched prior to their fall. Thanksgiving must be "how" we pray with them.

As we close this chapter, we must sincerely evaluate our prayer life. Ask...

- *Have I prayed with a grateful or a judgmental heart?*
- *Do I sincerely appreciate the people that God has brought into our care?*
- *Even in correction do they feel valued and appreciated?*
- *Have I prayed for spiritual leaders who have missed the mark with thanksgiving and interceded for them until they come out of their deception and error?*

Did you know that thanksgiving can bring health and restoration into your life and the lives of others? Let's discover how.

CHAPTER 6

Thanksgiving Brings Restoration and Health

One of the greatest examples of the power of thanksgiving from a grateful heart is that of the ten lepers in Luke 17. Leprosy was a disease common in the Middle East during the time of Jesus. My visit to a leper's colony over in the Philippines was one of the most impacting experiences of my entire life. In this remote island called Culion they had a hospital for people who had contacted leprosy. Many of the people had eyes that had been greatly enlarged from the disease. Others had lost fingers, hands, toes, and other body parts. As we went in to pray for one lady, she got up in bed and thanked us for coming. Then she told us they prayed for missionaries like us every day. Then she gave us a hug. She only had two stumps at the ends of her arms — no hands or fingers. I was incredibly moved by this experience because I sensed the love, faith, and heart of Jesus in the woman. Here I was in a foreign land and people are there strategically praying for us. That is incredible and overwhelming to me as we see God's love, not just for the people we minister to, but also for us.

The Jewish people of Jesus' day believed that leprosy was a disease put on people as punishment for sin and was a clear mark of God's displeasure towards the person. Today many are afflicted with AIDS from circumstances out of their control and are often treated with the same mentality instead of the compassion for them that Jesus had. I remember a few years back while I was speaking in Panama City at Hosanna Church. Every Wednesday the people would bring the AIDS victims to the church in the morning, and then intercession went up for them all day. That evening the minister preaching would lay hands on them. What an experience that was as I felt the compassion of Jesus flowing into them and the presence of God upon them.

God's will has never changed. Through His church today people can be set free, restored, and made whole, just as in the Bible days. The miracles, signs, and wonders in Acts were never meant to stop but to continue right on up until the return of Jesus.

The Ten Lepers

Now it happened as He went to Jerusalem that He passed through the midst of Samaria and Galilee. Then as He entered a certain village, there met Him ten men who were lepers, who stood afar off. And they lifted up their voices and said, "Jesus, Master, have mercy on us!" So when He saw them, He said to them, "Go, show yourselves to the priests." And so it was that as they went, they were cleansed. And one of them, when he saw that he was healed, returned, and with a loud voice glorified God, and fell down on his face at His feet, giving Him thanks. And he was a Samaritan. So Jesus answered and said, "Were there not ten cleansed? But where are the nine? Were there not any found who returned to give glory to God except this foreigner?" And He said to him, "Arise, go your way. Your faith has made you well." (Luke 17:11-19)

These ten lepers were all in one accord as they lifted up their voices to Jesus. They had to be a far way off because the disease was extremely contagious. During that time they had leper colonies oftentimes in caves, and family members would leave food at the foot of the leper colony for loved ones. The lepers did not ask to be healed, but that Jesus would have mercy on them, as the teaching of that day was that leprosy was a punishment for their sin. Jesus told them to go show themselves to the priest who was the one who would inspect them and pronounce them clean if they were cured of the disease. They all went and they all were cleansed of the disease. As they obeyed the command of Jesus to "go," they were cleansed.

The one man who came back to Jesus to give thanks is identified as a Samaritan, which implies that the other nine were Jews. Not only was this Samaritan man cleansed, he was also made whole, which means that the body parts affected by the leprosy were now made complete. Being cleansed of leprosy was an amazing thing to these men, but wholeness and restoration came to the one with a grateful heart. I wonder how many believers come to Jesus and are cleansed of their sin through the work of the Cross and the shed blood of Jesus, but have never learned that Jesus wants to restore their souls, minds, and bodies.

As we reflect on this amazing story of restoration, we need to accept the truth that thanksgiving activates the miraculous in our lives. This is a good time to ask ourselves who are the lepers around us that have been labeled as deserving their affliction because of sin in their lives:

- *Is it a single mom who is pregnant for the second time?*
- *Is it a hotheaded neighbor who can't control his temper?*
- *Is it a fallen leader who hurt you so badly that you can't stand to hear his name mentioned?*
- *Is it an ex-spouse who really did you in and you want to see them pay for it? Is it an in-law who just repulses you by their arrogance?*
- *Is it a coworker whom everyone talks about behind their back who is made to feel totally rejected?*

- *Is it a child who turned against his or her family and brought great shame and pain to the family?*

I am totally convinced after forty years of being in ministry that restoration is available to the one with a thankful heart who appreciates the work of the Cross. When we begin to realize how good and merciful God has been to us and how faithful He has been to us, even when we have been faithless, it should turn our complaining into thankfulness. Do we want to be whole in our marriages, in our families, and in our churches? Here is the summary key to remember here:

☞ **Thanksgiving will bring wholeness to all who come with a grateful heart.**

If we fail to be thankful, what will happen? Let's turn now to understanding the consequences of ungratefulness.

CHAPTER 7

The Destruction Caused by Murmuring and Complaining

One of the things Cathy and I enjoy doing in Windsor is going out to eat because we have so many wonderful places to eat, and the variety of places is amazing. Every couple of months, we go to one of Cathy's favorite spots—an Italian restaurant called Spago in Windsor on Erie Street, which is an Italian neighborhood with many great restaurants, specialty stores, and a bakery that is off the charts. One night we went to Spago for dinner; it's ambiance and atmosphere really sets the tone for a great night out. The waiters all dress in tuxedo-style suits and have a towel wrapped over their arm. They provide incredible, friendly service that makes you want to return over and over again.

One night the candles on the tables were burning, leaving a sweet aroma in the air, along with the smell of freshly baked bread with the sprinkles of rosemary and oregano and covered with fresh roasted garlic that melts in your mouth. Cathy and I were having a great night out; we were relaxed and enjoying one another. We ordered our favorite meal. We laughed and talked and just enjoyed each other until the waiter brought the check. I looked at it and without thinking just complained for a moment about how expensive it was. The very moment I murmured, I looked over at Cathy and her face was filled with disappointment. I asked, "What is the matter?"

"Nothing," she replied. I paid the bill and as we drove home, the car was filled with silence. When we arrived home, I felt that she was tense. I went to my downstairs study and she went upstairs. What I thought was going to be a romantic night turned out to be a life-changing moment for me as I began to pray. I felt grieved and to my amazement, I believe God's Holy Spirit in me was also grieved. As I sat and reflected, the Holy Spirit impressed me to review the evening's conversation. I recognized that I had shut my wife down and grieved her when I had complained. The Holy Spirit convicted me greatly and communicated that we as Christians often complain and stifle His joy and work in our lives. I saw very clearly that night that murmuring shuts down the Holy Spirit from guiding, revealing, sharing, illuminating, encouraging, comforting, helping, counseling, aiding, and ministering to us. What I realized was that murmuring was a manifestation of ungratefulness. Instead of rejoicing and thanking the Lord that we were in a position financially to go to a nice place like Spago once in a while to have a great meal and enjoy a relaxing evening, I had complained with an ungrateful heart. That murmuring had shut down me and my wife, and quenched the joy of the moment that the Holy Spirit had desired for us. I realized that every time I murmur or complain about something so trivial as a check after a meal, I can literally shut down God's best for my life.

How many people every day murmur and complain about their finances, job, family, spouse, boss, government, the weather, and on and on? Such ungrateful complaining hinders the work of His Spirit in us. I wonder how many of us have taken the blessing of the Lord for granted and over time became unappreciative? I wonder how many spouses are reading this book right now and reflecting on their conversations with one another. In fact, you may have killed a wonderful evening together with your negativity about others or situations. You, with your spouse, may want to stop reading for a moment and pray: *Heavenly Father, help us to begin to appreciate the blessing of the Lord over and upon our lives. Help us, Father, to appreciate the gifts that You have given to us in our spouse, children, and family members. Father God, help us to put aside all murmuring and complaining and to exchange them for praising and thanksgiving. In Jesus' name, Amen.*

Two of the most deadly words in the Bible are "murmuring" and "complaining," yet they are commonly spoken and culturally accepted in most of the church world today. We have been learning that thanksgiving is the doorway into the miraculous, the supernatural, and is effective in the spirit realm. The opposite of thanksgiving is complaining, and I am convinced it is the doorway into hell, oppression, and releases the kingdom of darkness.

Murmur means a mumbled or private expression of discontent, to complain in a low tone or in private. *Complain* means to express dissatisfaction, pain, uneasiness, censure, resentment, or grief; to criticize and find fault. *Synonyms* for complaining are grumbling, growling, and whining.

In Philippians 2:14-16, Paul writes in strong terms concerning complaining and arguing among believers. "Do all things without complaining and disputing, that you may become blameless and harmless, children of God without fault in the midst of a crooked and perverse generation, among whom you shine as lights in the world, holding fast the word of life, so that I may rejoice in the day of Christ that I have not run in vain or labored in vain". Paul recognized that if the church was to advance, grow, and become influential, the complaining and arguing had to go.

I have learned that murmuring and complaining invites, activates, releases, empowers, connects, and houses the demons of Satan in our lives. Demons are legalistic and capitalize on every opportunity they can, using the words that come out of our mouths. So much oppression, sickness, bondage, anger, fear, and hatred come from root issues of murmuring and complaining.

➻ **Thanksgiving and a grateful heart activate, release, empower, connect, and house the Holy Spirit and angels in our lives.**

"Do **all** things **without**" means doing everything we do with the absence, omission, or avoidance of something; in this case without complaining and arguing. Notice that the results of avoiding complaining and arguing make us blameless or irreproachable. It also says we will be harmless, which here means without a mixture of evil, making us pure children of God, without fault, even though we are living in the midst of a crooked and perverse generation.

➻ **When we refuse to grumble and complain, we shine as lights in the crooked and perverse generation in which we live.**

Murmuring Is Contagious

Murmuring is the most contagious of all spiritual diseases. Something about murmuring becomes so perilous that it spreads quickly and poisons everyone who is contaminated by it.

➻ **Murmuring is a spiritual disease in the church world that has arrested successful prayer and often goes virtually undetected.**

In his letter to the Philippians, Paul needs to bring correction to a problem of murmuring that is becoming contagious in that church. But before Paul addresses the problem he follows his pattern of introducing the element of thanksgiving first. Philippians 1:1-3 says, "Paul and Timotheus, the servants of Jesus Christ, to all the saints in Christ Jesus which are at Philippi, with the bishops and deacons: Grace be unto you, and peace, from God our Father, and from the Lord Jesus Christ. **I thank my God upon every remembrance of you.**"

Paul then brings correction to the church, and in particular, two women, Euodia and Syntyche, who argued about some point of doctrine. He encourages them to be of the same mind, but also to rejoice always in the Lord. Correction is more readily accepted in an atmosphere of thanksgiving. It tends to assuage the hearer, making each one feel valued. In verse four, Paul writes, "In all my prayers for all of you, I always pray with joy" (NIV). God responds to this thankful, joyous attitude in the same way that we do. We enjoy the company of grateful, happy people. Paul recognizes that he must exercise the fruit of the Spirit in this situation. He also knows that God inhabits the praises of His people and he needs God's attention and wisdom to direct the saints.

Properly Expressing Concerns

If we examine the life of David we notice that he brings his complaints or concerns to God, but always ends with praise and thanksgiving. Even with numerous threats against his life, David chooses to respect the office of the king and spares Saul's life. He warns Abishai, "Destroy him not; for who can stretch forth his hand against the Lord's anointed and be guiltless?" (1 Samuel 26:9 KJV) David realizes that he has to change his heart towards Saul to get results in prayer.

If I come home and complain about something that happened during the day, my wife stops me immediately. She has little patience for grumbling and whining. The complaints can be situations I brought upon myself or issues over which I have no control. For example, there is no profit in grumbling about poorly timed streetlights, careless drivers, or gas prices. Grumblers are poor company. They are like a cold front stealing the warmth of a summer's day. Who wants to be around someone who complains about his job, his car, his children, or his city? Our society caters to murmurers. Newspapers, radio, and television talk programs encourage readers and listeners to voice their complaints. Issues involving government, politics, and taxes generate huge audience appeal.

When we feel the urge to whine over a matter we need to stop and ask this question: Will my grumbling and complaining change the situation? If not, save yourself and everyone else the aggravation of this negative behavior. Instead, intentionally focus on all the things for which you are thankful for, such as faith, friends, family, and health, to name a few. Your thanksgiving will change the atmosphere in which you live and bring blessing to God.

When Windsor Christian Fellowship first started, there were many financial and administrative challenges. Another church gave us a small photocopier which produced one copy every eighty seconds. It took over five minutes for the thing to heat up.

However, I was grateful to God and that church for the gift. Our current $50,000 copier creates books, stapled, collated, and punched. It's great, but I really think that I was more thankful for that small photocopier that arrived in the beginning of our ministry just when we needed it. I don't take that for granted.

The Bible gives us practical ways to handle life's everyday events that might tempt us to murmur or complain. For example, when guests are coming over to your home and they make a mess of the house, eat all your food, and stay longer than originally planned, what do you do? The answer is found in 1 Peter 4:9-10, "Be hospitable to one another without grumbling. As each one has received a gift, minister it to one another, as good stewards of the manifold grace of God."

Another area we need to handle in a godly manner is faultfinding against one another in the Body of Christ. James 5:9 provides our answer for this one, "Do not grumble against one another, brethren, lest you be condemned."

Negativity, A Modern Plague

We live in a media world that is extremely negative and we find the more bad news they report, the more media they sell. The more scandalous the situation, the more people tune into their radio or TV stations to hear about it. The more sickening the story the more the talk shows promote it. It's a negative and warped society that you and I are called to shine as bright lights in. Negativity is the root of murmuring and complaining. Negativity is a modern plague in the life of many of God's people that goes unchallenged and causes great damage to those it comes in contact with. It contaminates, pollutes, and sours people's perspective of one another.

Negativity means to negate, to nullify, neutralize, prohibit, declare nonexistent, make empty, render invalid, counterreact, and destroy. Synonyms for negativity are unconstructiveness, unhelpfulness, pessimism and disapproval. The opposite of negativity is enthusiasm. Negativity verbalizes inner defeat that focuses on its weaknesses, failures, and shortcomings.

Understand that negativity lashes out with criticism, judgment, harshness, and resentment— especially towards people who are moving ahead, winning, successful, and living Godly, productive lives. It thrives on self-pity, has a victim mentality, and is plagued by failure and defeat. Negativity is characterized by excuses, blame, and finger-pointing, and produces mediocre relationships; it destroys marriages, families, churches, schools, governments, businesses, and teamwork. Finally, negativity poisons all that it touches by infecting people with cynicism and discontentment, and manifests as a spirit of pride, which is the very character of Lucifer himself.

How do we overcome a negative, critical, murmuring, and complaining spirit? Jude, the stepbrother of Jesus, gives us the answer:

These are grumblers, complainers, walking according to their own lusts; and they mouth great swelling words, flattering people to gain advantage. But you, beloved, remember the words which were spoken before by the apostles of our Lord Jesus Christ: how they told you that there would be mockers in the last time who would walk according to their own ungodly lusts. These are sensual persons, who cause divisions, not having the Spirit. **But you, beloved, building yourselves up on your most holy faith, praying in the Holy Spirit, keep yourselves in the love of God, looking for the mercy of our Lord Jesus Christ unto eternal life.** (Jude 16-21)

Thanksgiving builds, strengthens, and fortifies us, while complaining tears down relationships; a grateful heart recognizes our need for God and releases faith so our prayers bring about change. Thanksgiving keeps us in the love and mercy of God as it focuses on eternal life. May each of us today realize that thanksgiving releases the Kingdom Life to those around us! Here's the Kingdom key:

☙ **Gratitude is contagious, and Heaven waits for our response to His work of the Cross through living a thankful life for Him.**

Ready for a breakthrough in your own life out of grumbling and complaining? Okay, then be ready to be "hot," not "lukewarm," in thanksgiving. How? Read on!

CHAPTER 8

Breaking Out of Complacency and Ingratitude

Many years ago I was out for dinner with a group of leaders after a conference, and I heard complaint after complaint about the cities they pastored in: how the ground was hard, their people didn't care about the things of God, and more general negative statements about their communities. It was evident that day why their ministries were hindered and not growing at all because of their ungrateful attitudes. I thought the people were amazing and incredibly hungry for the things of God, but ingratitude had blinded them from seeing the precious gems in their midst.

I remember one time in my home church in Windsor when there was a very high maintenance individual who needed a lot of time and attention. A leader was complaining about this person to me, and to my surprise this came out of my mouth, "If it wasn't for people like this, you wouldn't have a job." Oftentimes we take for granted people around us, and ingratitude hinders us from connecting and ministering to them. However, when we are grateful for the opportunities to love the unlovable and help hurting people, we are showing our gratefulness for what God has done in our lives.

I believe the root cause of being lukewarm in our spiritual lives is ingratitude. We see a reference to this in the church at Laodicea in Revelation 3:14-22 that many scholars believe will be the description of the Body of Christ before Jesus returns:

And to the angel of the church of the Laodiceans write, "These things says the Amen, the Faithful and True Witness, the Beginning of the creation of God: 'I know your works, that you are neither cold nor hot. I could wish you were cold or hot. So then, because you are lukewarm, and neither cold nor hot, I will vomit you out of My mouth. Because you say, I am rich, have become wealthy, and have need of nothing—and do not know that you are wretched, miserable, poor, blind, and naked—I counsel you to buy from Me gold refined in the fire, that you may be rich; and white garments, that you may be clothed, that the shame of your nakedness may not be revealed; and anoint your eyes with eye salve, that you may see. As many as I love, I rebuke and chasten. Therefore be zealous and repent. Behold, I stand at the door and knock. If anyone hears My voice and opens the door, I will come in to him and dine with him, and he with Me. To him who overcomes I will grant to sit with Me on My throne, as I also overcame and sat down with My Father on His throne. He who has an ear, let him hear what the Spirit says to the churches." (Revelation 3:14-22)

My writing of this chapter is not to teach on end-times but on how this church had arrived at such a complacent, deceived, and lukewarm state. What many are not aware of is that Laodicea was mentioned in five other places in the Word of God in the New Testament Epistles. What was written to them apparently was not practiced or heeded so they ended up this way. So many believers today start off well until bumps in their journey cause them to hit some tough times, or temptations come to lure them away and they lose their passion for the things of God. They begin to pursue mammon or worldliness and they become mediocre or lukewarm in their relationship with the Lord.

The other references to this church are found in the Book of Colossians and in the beginning of the Book of Revelation. Revelation 1:10-11 reads, "I was in the Spirit on the Lord's Day, and I heard behind me a loud voice, as of a trumpet, saying, 'I am the Alpha and the Omega, the First and the Last,' and, 'What you see, write in a book and send it to the seven churches which are in Asia: to Ephesus, to Smyrna, to Pergamos, to Thyatira, to Sardis, to Philadelphia, and to **Laodicea.**'" Jesus was issuing warnings and admonishments to all of these churches through His servant John. But I want to focus on the four references to Laodicea in the book of Colossians that led this church to end up in their lukewarm condition.

- **Colossians 2:1-3** reads, "For I want you to know what a great conflict I have for you and those in **Laodicea,** and for as many as have not seen my face in the flesh, that their hearts may be encouraged, being knit together in love, and attaining to all riches of the full assurance of understanding, to the knowledge of the mystery of God, both of the Father and of Christ, in whom are hidden all the treasures of wisdom and knowledge."
- **Colossians 4:12-17** reveals, "Epaphras, who is one of you, a bondservant of Christ, greets you, always laboring fervently for you in prayers, that you may stand perfect and complete in all the will of God. For I bear him witness that he has a great zeal for you, and those who are in **Laodicea,** and those in Hierapolis. Luke the beloved physician and Demas greet you. Greet the brethren who are in **Laodicea,** and Nymphas and the church that is in his house. Now when this epistle is read among you, see that it is read also in the church of the **Laodiceans,** and that you likewise read the epistle from **Laodicea.** And say to Archippus,

'Take heed to the ministry which you have received in the Lord, that you may fulfill it.'"

In these two passages, we learn that the Apostle Paul and Epaphras were in a great inward conflict or struggle and burdened for the saints in Colosse and also those in Laodicea. We see Demas mentioned, who was a coworker of Paul's but who later abandoned the faith because of worldly attachments (see 2 Timothy 4:10). What was it in the Epistle to the Colossians that was a strong warning to the church at Laodicea? I believe there is a central theme interwoven into every chapter that they did not heed and ultimately lost their passion and fervency. That theme was gratefulness, thanksgiving, and the giving of thanks.

The Book of Colossians on Thankfulness

Colossians 1:3 says, "We give thanks to the God and Father of our Lord Jesus Christ, praying always for you." One of the first things Paul does when he addresses the church is give thanks, which we have learned is sanctifying the atmosphere for the Holy Ghost to work in. Next we see in Paul's thankful prayer to the Father, who has qualified us to be partakers/sharers/coparticipants in the inheritance of the saints of light in Colossians 1:12-13. Next we see Paul telling them to abound in faith with thanksgiving: "As you therefore have received Christ Jesus the Lord, so walk in Him, rooted and built up in Him and established in the faith, as you have been taught, abounding in it with thanksgiving" (Colossians 2:6-7).

Abounding means to exceed over and above a fixed number or measure; it isn't a hit and miss type thing, but something that is constantly before their eyes to focus upon. In this case Paul says they are to abound in gratitude.

The very next verse says, "Beware lest anyone cheat you through philosophy and empty deceit, according to the tradition of men, according to the basic principles of the world, and not according to Christ" (Colossians 2:8).

☞ **Thanksgiving will keep you from error, deceptive philosophies, and human traditions that make the Word of God of no effect.**

How many Christians have gotten sidetracked onto various tangents and philosophies that caused them to deviate from and shipwreck their faith in God? This is a very real danger for Christians, and being thankful for your local church, for those who brought you to Christ, and for the Body of Christ as a whole, will keep you safe from these side issues. The world is characterized by negativity, misery, complaining, murmuring, and discontentment; but Christianity is characterized by being positive, thinking on good things and good reports, being joyful, voicing thanksgiving, and being content with the place God has led us to worship and the family into which He has placed us.

In all circumstances and situations, in all that you do and say, give thanks to God.

Then Paul again shares his advice on how to stay on track amidst the activities of daily life: "Whatsoever ye do in word or deed, do all in the name of the Lord Jesus, giving thanks to God and the Father by Him" (Colossians 3:17 KJV). That means whether you're going to work, washing the car, paying your bills, or changing the child's diapers, you are to give thanks. While you're working overtime, giving your tithes and offering, going grocery shopping, or going to the health club to exercise, you should be giving thanks. At all meal times, whether at home or dining out, give thanks.

Whether you live in a house, an apartment, a trailer, a condo, or a rented room, you give thanks for the blessing of a roof over your head. Giving thanks for the leaders of your church, your supervisors at work, and all other authorities in your life gives you a continual attitude of gratitude as you move through your day. Whether your children are young and living at home or grown and married, give thanks to God for the blessings they are in your life.

A word of wisdom for married couples: Wives who have a hard time submitting to their husbands are wives that are not thankful for their husbands:

ꬶ Ingratitude in the marriage relationship causes a separation of the affections to take place.

Husbands, love your wives, and be not bitter against them. Husbands who are holding grudges, resentments, and ill will towards their wives are ungrateful for them, and the ungratefulness blocks the favor of God from flowing into their marriage. He who finds a wife finds a good thing and obtains favor from the Lord. If you are making fun of your wife and putting her down to your peers, you are canceling out God's favor from your life (1 Peter 3:7). Wives who complain and murmur about their husbands are blocking the blessing of God from coming to their household. Neither the husband or wife will have their prayers answered, and they will both be frustrated with each other until thankfulness comes back into their relationship and sweeps the atmosphere clean.

If couples would just remember the vows they made at the altar and begin to remember the good times and cultivate gratefulness for each other, God could have a more active role in their families. Couples' prayers would have great force in the spirit realm and results in victories in the natural realm if they would remember that whatever they do in word or deed, do it in the name of Lord, giving thanks to God.

Colossians 4:2 teaches, "Continue earnestly in prayer, being vigilant in it with thanksgiving." In our prayer time we are to be vigilant or watchful, but notice again, with thanksgiving. God tells us to devote ourselves to prayer, being watchful and thankful.

Prayers that are not from a grateful heart will not be answered. God is not responsible to answer prayers that are requested from a wrong spirit or motive. This is reinforced in Philippians 4:6 as well: "Be careful for nothing; but in everything by prayer and supplication with thanksgiving let your requests be made known unto God" (KJV). Our prayers are to be *with* thanksgiving. The word "with" means accompaniment or together, so all of our requests and prayers must be accompanied by or joined together with thanksgiving.

It is my personal opinion that many prayers that are released into the atmosphere today are nothing more than selfish and demonic, which release the spirit of witchcraft towards those the prayer is being sent to.

☛ **Wives and husbands who complain about their spouses and pray for God to change them, break them, melt them, and mold them, are trying to control and manipulate rather than improve their relationships. There is truly no gratitude expressed in their prayers.**

Thanksgiving permeates through the entire epistle of Colossians, which Paul said was also to be read to the church at Laodicea. A few years later the church at Laodicea had lost its fire because they had become ungrateful for the work of the Cross, ungrateful for the Body of Christ, and ungrateful in how God had blessed them. They had begun to take for granted all the blessings of God. This brings the rebuke from the Lord for their lukewarmness.

Ingratitude and Its Consequences

Ingratitude is the state of being ungrateful or unthankful. We saw the example of the ten lepers, who were cleansed of their disease as they went in faith by Jesus' words. Only one came back with gratitude and he was a Samaritan. How many Christians do the same thing? God blesses them, prospers them, restores something back to them, and they never even thank Him. It's as if they feel it's something owed to them or an entitlement.

☞ An attitude of entitlement fosters ingratitude.

This is the opposite of the character of God. Jesus said in Luke 6:35-36, "But love your enemies, do good, and lend, hoping for nothing in return; and your reward will be great, and you will be sons of the Most High. For He is kind to the unthankful and evil. Therefore be merciful, just as your Father also is merciful." Notice God is kind to the unthankful and evil. God loves lost humanity. Jesus taught this through His parables in Luke 15: the Parable of the Lost Sheep, the Parable of the Lost Coin, and the Parable of the Lost Son. Apparently lost people matter to the Lord, and should to us also.

God Chasers

In Paul's letters to his spiritual son Timothy, who was pastoring a megachurch in Ephesus, he writes about the conditions that will be prevalent in the last days' church: "But know this, that in the last days perilous times will come: For men will be lovers of themselves, lovers of money, boasters, proud, blasphemers, disobedient to parents, **unthankful,** unholy, unloving, unforgiving, slanderers, without self-control, brutal, despisers of good, traitors, headstrong, haughty, lovers of pleasure rather than lovers of God, having a form of godliness but denying its power. And from such people turn away!" (2 Timothy 3:1-5).

Notice right smack in the middle he mentions they will be unthankful, which means ungrateful, thankless, and unappreciative of favorable things that have happened in one's life. We should not be surprised about the warning that Paul gave prophetically to the church that people would be self-centered and unthankful. How accurate these words are today as we see end-times events unfolding all around us.

I believe that ungratefulness shuts off the power of God in a believer's life. Paul says this end-times church will have a form of godliness, but denying its power. God's Word even tells us not to hang with these types of people. He warns us to turn away from them and avoid them.

☞ Avoid associating with ungrateful people!

I have been praying and meditating on how ingratitude inhibits the church and our lives.

I wonder...

- *what the church would be like if we heeded His Word and avoided the lovers of self who were only concerned about what they can get out of church rather than what they can give to the church?*
- *what the church would look like if every believer faithfully brought their tithe and offering to the house of the Lord and broke that spirit of covetousness and lack of fear of the Lord which tithing teaches us?*
- *what the church would look like if a spirit of humility and submission was present in the leaders and ran right down to every member?*
- *if miracles, signs, and wonders would be more prevalent in our corporate gatherings if every believer came to church with a grateful heart to worship, praise, and thank the Lord?*
- *if we would see God's glory revealed in the earth through His church if we became God chasers in every aspect of our lives and had more of the fear of the Lord, were more loving, more forgiving, less critical, and operated with a kindness that was supernaturally from God?*
- *if His power would be demonstrated to all of those in need if His church remained teachable, humble, and heeded the warning given us in Paul's letter to Timothy?*

The Message of the Cross

"For the wrath of God is revealed from heaven against all ungodliness and unrighteousness of men, who suppress the truth in unrighteousness, because what may be known of God is manifest in them, for God has shown it to them. For since the creation of the world His invisible attributes are clearly seen, being understood by the things that are made, even His eternal power and Godhead, so that **they are without excuse,** because, **although they knew God, they did not glorify Him as God, nor were thankful,** but **became** futile in their thoughts, and their foolish hearts were darkened" (Romans 1:18-21).

God has shown man His invisible attributes and made sure humanity had a way to understand His eternal power. Man has been given what he needs to live a life of godliness, so he is without excuse. We see the downhill spiral that man sets himself on when he begins to operate from an unthankful, ungrateful heart. These people knew God but became futile in their thoughts. It did not happen all of a sudden or overnight, but through a process of time. Futile means useless or ineffective. These were individuals, who at one time or another walked with God and had something happen to them that caused them to turn away from God.

Their thinking, imaginations, and inward reasoning became empty and futile. These are all the problems that unthankful people begin to experience. They begin inwardly trying to reason everything out rather than to live by faith. When we begin to try to rationalize, reason, and manipulate how God works and moves, we fall from faith and grace and become vain and carnal. Proverbs 3:5 says, "Trust in the Lord with all thine heart, and lean not unto thine own understanding" (KJV).

Ungrateful thinking leads to questioning about what is true. They question whether things clearly outlined in the Word of God are still relevant today; like giving, tithing, serving, going to church, and operating in the fivefold gifts. They begin to build walls of indifference and separate from the Body of Christ, which leaves their minds open to deception. Ungrateful people become double-minded and start doubting their faith, their salvation, their morals, and standards of belief. They stop praying because they don't believe that God is going to answer their prayers anyway. They begin to try to prove to others their conclusions as their hearts become darkened.

People whose hearts have become darkened see things through dark sunglasses. "Darkened" means to obscure or cover with darkness. It is also used to describe ignorance in respect to divine things and human duties. As things become obscured they can't see things clearly anymore. They yield to whatever the flesh or the sensual demonic realm tells them.

Look at these two Scriptures as they show us the result of the obscured vision or sight. In Matthew 6:21-23, Jesus said, "For where your treasure is, there your heart will be also. The lamp of the body is the eye. If therefore your eye is good, your whole body will be full of light. But if your eye is bad, your whole body will be full of darkness. If therefore the light that is in you is darkness, how great is that darkness!" Then Paul says in Titus 1:15, "To the pure all things are pure, but to those who are defiled and unbelieving nothing is pure; but even their mind and conscience are defiled."

Once this darkness clouds our way of thinking, the enemy gets us into pride, deception, and error. Romans 1:22-23 warns us of the consequences of such a darkened heart: "Professing to be wise, they became fools, and changed the glory of the incorruptible God into an image made like corruptible man—and birds and four-footed animals and creeping things." They claim they are wise, but the beginning of wisdom is the fear of the Lord, which they have now exchanged for a lie. As a result, they become fools. It is so important for believers to remain in thanksgiving at all times and for all things. This is the antidote for deception. A grateful heart creates an atmosphere for God to invade the darkness and clouded thinking with a clear revelation of the truth.

Old Testament Examples of the Consequences of Ingratitude

King David, the writer of many of the Psalms, understood the importance of a thankful heart. Psalm 69:30-31 says, "I will praise the name of God with a song, and will magnify him with thanksgiving. This also shall please the Lord better than (the sacrifice of) an ox or bullock" (KJV).

Though David understood this principle of total worship and giving thanks to God, his wife, Michal, did not. Read the conversation between David and Michal in 2 Samuel 6:20-23:

Then David returned to bless his household. And Michal the daughter of Saul came out to meet David, and said, "How glorious was the king of Israel today, uncovering himself today in the eyes of the maids of his servants, as one of the base fellows shamelessly uncovers himself!" So David said to Michal, "It was before the Lord, who chose me instead of your father and all his house, to appoint me ruler over the people of the Lord, over Israel. Therefore I will play music before the Lord. And I will be even more undignified than this, and will be humble in my own sight. But as for the maidservants of whom you have spoken, by them I will be held in honor." Therefore Michal the daughter of Saul had no children to the day of her death.

God longs for this type of worshipper today who will come with gratitude and appreciation for all His blessings, goodness, provision, protection, and faithfulness to us. "Michal" means one who is like God, which speaks to us today of religion without a relationship. This type of religion is always speaking out in a judgmental, critical, jealous, and unthankful way.

☞ The result of this ungratefulness is lack of productivity or barrenness.

Michal let her pride get in the way. I believe that deep down inside she wanted to behave and dance just like her husband because God has put that desire into each of us. Little children love to dance, play, and enjoy life, which is the way God made each and every one of us. Unthankful people like Michal are not happy people; they have no joy and have great difficulty seeing beyond their little world.

King David was so overcome by the goodness of the Lord that he couldn't stop himself from expressing thanksgiving to the Lord. The amazing point is that David came down and worshipped with the common everyday people of his kingdom. This was very upsetting to David's wife, just as it upsets many today in the church world. God, the ultimate ruler of the universe, wants to dwell with the ordinary, common, everyday believer, and make them a part of His royal family. Is not that what Jesus did with us? He left His throne and came down and lived among us, accepted us, blessed us, and called us to be a part of the royal family of God. He called us to eat at His table and enjoy being made a royal priesthood and holy nation. Thanksgiving is a natural high that depression, fear, negative stress, and grumblers can't stand to be around.

When we keep our focus on the Cross, then we will not forget or devalue the anguish, suffering, pain, punishment, hatred, sin, rebellion, and disobedience that Jesus took on Himself on that Cross. Paul warns us in Galatians 6:14 not to neglect this powerful, foundational truth: "But God forbid that I should boast except in the Cross of our Lord Jesus Christ, by whom the world has been crucified to me, and I to the world." The New Living Translation reads, "As for me, I never boast about anything except the Cross of our Lord Jesus Christ. Because of that Cross, my interest in the world has been crucified, and the world's interest in me has also died." How foreign are these words in the church world today.

Foolish men have said the Cross is the place of defeat, which means they are perishing, according to 1 Corinthians 1:18: "For the message of the Cross is foolishness to those who are perishing, but to us who are being saved it is the power of God."

→ **We need to offer God a sacrifice of thanksgiving as we worship Him for paying it all, giving His all, and empowering us to do His works in the earth today.**

When we consistently do this, we will not have to suffer the consequences of an ungrateful, darkened heart. Now I want to share with you a special place of thanksgiving open for all believers.

CHAPTER 9

Thanksgiving in Communion

One of the most special times around Windsor Christian Fellowship is when we break bread at Holy Communion. After we have worshiped, taught the Word, and baptized people in the name of the Father, Son, and Holy Spirit, we have a precious time of Communion among our fellow believers. Many times at Communion, the Lord will share prophetically words of knowledge, words of wisdom, and prophecy as we sense His Presence in a powerful way. The early church word for Communion is *eucharist,* which literally means "to be thankful, grateful, to give thanks." In churches with liturgical worship, Communion is called the *Eucharist.*

Just a few weeks ago a word came during Communion that was very strong: "Stop It; you're leaving your spouse and God says, 'Stop It.' " Amazingly, a week later a woman met me in the visitor's room with her husband and children. She said she had come to WCF for the first time the previous weekend and was planning to file divorce papers on Monday. When she heard the words *stop it*, she knew it was a direct message for her from God. She had brought her husband and children the following Sunday and they all gave their lives to the Lord. They are working on their marriage to the glory of God.

Communion means partnership, participation, fellowship, association, community, joint participation, and intimacy. Communion is found seven times in Scriptures and four of them are the same account written by Matthew, Mark, Luke, and Paul. I have learned that if the same story is mentioned twice in the Word of God, then it is something we are to really take heed of. If the story is mentioned three times, then it must really be important to the Lord that we have understanding on it. But when the Word of God repeats the same message four times, it means this is pivotal for your success and well-being as a Christian.

Communion

Read the following passages out loud. After each one, say a short prayer of thanksgiving to Christ Jesus for His broken body and shed blood:

> *"And as they were eating, Jesus took bread,*
> *blessed and broke it,*
> *and gave it to the disciples and said,*
> *'Take, eat; this is My body.'"*
> (Matthew 26:26)

"And as they were eating, Jesus took bread,
blessed and broke it,
and gave it to them and said, 'Take, eat;
this is My body.'"
(Mark 14:22)

"And He took bread, gave thanks and broke it,
and gave it to them, saying,
'This is My body which is given for you;
do this in remembrance of Me.'"
(Luke 22:19)

"Now it came to pass, as He sat at the table with
them, that He took bread,
blessed and broke it, and gave it to them.
Then their eyes were opened and they knew Him;
and He vanished from their sight."
(Luke 24:30-31)

"And as day was about to dawn, Paul implored
them all to take food,
saying, 'Today is the fourteenth day you have
waited and continued without food,
and eaten nothing. Therefore I urge you to take
nourishment, for this is for your survival,
since not a hair will fall from the head
of any of you.'
And when he had said these things, he took bread
and gave thanks to God
in the presence of them all; and when he had
broken it he began to eat.

Then they were all encouraged, and also
took food themselves.
And in all we were two hundred and seventy-six
persons on the ship.
So when they had eaten enough, they lightened the
ship and threw out the wheat into the sea."
(Acts 27:33-38)

"The cup of blessing which we bless, is it not the
communion of the blood of Christ?
The bread which we break, is it not the communion
of the body of Christ?
For we, though many, are one bread and one body;
for we all partake of that one bread."
(1 Corinthians 10:16-17)

"For I received from the Lord that which I also
delivered to you:
that the Lord Jesus on the same night in which He
was betrayed took bread;
and when He had given thanks,
He broke it and said,
'Take, eat; this is My body which is broken for you;
do this in remembrance of Me.'
In the same manner He also took the cup
after supper, saying,
'This cup is the new covenant in My blood.
This do, as often as you drink it,
in remembrance of Me.' For as often as you
eat this bread and drink this cup,
you proclaim the Lord's death till He comes."
(1 Corinthians 11:23-26)

In all of these accounts, the Last Supper was held on the night in which Judas betrayed Christ and sold Him out for thirty pieces of silver. Betrayal is probably the most painful thing to the inside of a person. Many who have been betrayed never get over it and others have been spiritually crippled, paralyzed, and stopped in their faith afterwards. The dictionary tells us that *betrayal* means to deliver or expose to an enemy by treachery or disloyalty, to disappoint the hopes or expectations of, to seduce and desert, and to disclose a secret, confidence, in violation of trust.

Many years ago, one of our children was violated by a babysitter whom we had entrusted to watch our child. When this happens to your family, all kinds of negative emotions and pain hits your mind, and you want vengeance to take place on the one that violated your child. This was one of the most painful times in my life. I had just become a Christian and was really fighting unforgiveness against the perpetrator. I did so with God's grace, and years later lead that individual to Christ. We did, however, put up a strong boundary that this person would never be allowed to be with any of our children alone at any time. Some say that is not forgiveness, but they are ignorant and fail to realize that nowhere in the Bible does it say forgiveness means that we will never remember what happened. It does say that the sting of betrayal will not have a place to control or hinder our life again.

Jesus was betrayed by one of His closest friends, Judas, who had also been entrusted with the finances of Jesus' ministry. When someone handles your finances, there has to be some real trust. What did Jesus do in the night in which He was betrayed?

"He took bread and when He had given thanks...." I believe Jesus had this recorded eight times for us in Scripture, four times in taking the bread and four times when He took the cup and gave thanks, because He was showing us the path to take when betrayal hits our lives.

In the Old Testament tabernacle, bread signified God's presence (Exodus 25:30). In the hours prior to His arrest, we can see that Jesus chose again and again to come into His Father's presence rather than focus on the impending betrayal. He could have responded in any number of negative ways, but instead, He chose to remain in the presence of God. He took bread and gave thanks. He refused to go to the Cross with bitterness in His heart toward His betrayer, or with complaints on His lips. Instead, He maintained a heart of thankfulness toward God.

Jesus took bread and gave thanks; He took His focus off what Judas did and came into the presence of His Father. The word *bread* literally means "the bread of His Presence or Bread of His Face." Jesus' words and actions were reminders of the High Priest of old who would take the table of showbread and commune with God. This is what Jesus did when He was betrayed. He didn't stay and focus on what the betrayer had done but came into the Father's presence and face. As He did so in faith, the sting of the betrayal had no more power over His life and He was able to willing lay down His life for the sins of the whole world.

What would happen if believers who had been betrayed would come quickly into the Father's presence and see their Heavenly Father's outstretched arms reaching towards them? What if we focused on His eyes of mercy and forgiveness instead of what had happened to us or a loved one?

➥ **When betrayed, a believer has the privilege of coming quickly into God's presence to receive the power of His loving forgiveness and mercy for the betrayer.**

The sting of the betrayal would be less and less every day as we come into His Presence. This truth has helped thousands of people over the years who had been spiritually paralyzed by betrayal. Thanksgiving coming out of Jesus' lips sanctified His Body to be laid down for the every man and woman on the planet, from then right up until today. There is so much power in thanksgiving.

Every time we break bread and drink of the cup we are to give thanks for the Cross of Christ because Scripture says by doing so we show His death until He comes. Death is the process to live the abundant life that Jesus said He came to bring those who would believe and receive. You can never separate the death, burial, and resurrection of Jesus, for they are all one event in the eyes of the Father. Someone had to die so that we can live. Now when we lose our lives, we find His life in us. When we give it comes back to us, but we have to release the gift first.

☛ **When we face trials, adversity, challenges, and betrayals in life, thanksgiving will clear the way for the sting to subside, and Christ's victory to be released upon our lives.**

Jesus Christ demonstrated the highest form of faith in the entire Word of God when He gave thanks in the night in which He was betrayed. This was not easy, this was not His emotion speaking, but it was what was in His heart. He had to come into the presence of the only One who could help Him in His time of need, His Heavenly Father. It is the same way for us today because Jesus opened the way for us to come before the throne of grace.

"For we do not have a High Priest who cannot
sympathize with our weaknesses,
but was in all points tempted as we are,
yet without sin.
Let us therefore come boldly to the throne of grace,
that we may obtain mercy and find grace
to help in time of need."
(Hebrews 4:15-16)

What is the need in your life right now? What is the difficulty you're facing at this moment? What is the urgent thing that is weighing you down even as you're reading this chapter? Stop and come before Him with a sacrifice of thanksgiving, not for what has happened, but for the solution out of it. As you do your burden will get lighter and lighter; just stay focused on Him face-to-face.

FINAL WORD

Live Thanksgiving

In our daily walk or lifestyle with God, it is so important for each one of us to finish well. *Walk* means to live as a way of life. We are to maintain a course of action conformed to God's will and that is pleasing in His sight. *Walk* speaks of our behavior and our conduct as we pursue the course of life set before each of us. Enoch walked with God for three hundred years, and the Lord took him up without subjecting him to physical death. That must have been a powerful walk of faith!

The New Testament gives us twelve exhortations of how our walk and life as believers can become fruitful.

>   *#1 - walk in newness of life*
>   *#2 - walk in faith*
>   *#3 - walk in love*
>   *#4 - walk circumspectly, diligently, accurately.*
>   *#5 - walk in the truth*

#6 - walk in wisdom
#7 - walk after the Spirit
#8 - walk honestly
#9 - walk in good works
#10 - walk after His commandments
#11 - walk in sanctification
#12 - walk as children of light

Every one of these can be accomplished as we practice the principle of thanksgiving first.

When we are close to God and are thankful, He responds. God is looking for us to initiate this relationship towards Him. There are seasons in the spiritual realm. There is a season to sow and a season to reap. We don't like the winter season, so many of us fly south. However, vacations soon end, and we have to return to face the cold. In the seasons of spiritual things we cannot escape the winter; there is no eternal summer, not in this life anyway. There are times when we must endure the winter times because it brings fruitfulness and maturity in the spring

And above all these things put on charity, which is the bond of perfectness. And let the peace of God rule in your hearts, to the which also ye are called in one body; **and be ye thankful.** *Let the word of Christ dwell in you richly in all wisdom; teaching and admonishing one another in psalms and hymns and spiritual songs, singing with grace in your hearts to the Lord. And whatsoever ye do in word or deed, do all in the name of the Lord*

Jesus, giving thanks to God and the Father by him. (Colossians 3:14-17 KJV)

☛ **Walk with Christ Jesus, filled with thanksgiving in every trial and test, in every circumstance and situation, on every mountaintop and through every valley.**

As you reach the end of this book, there is a tendency to put it down and forget about it, but I pray that the simple truths of this book would be applied daily in your life, marriage, home, family, church, marketplace, ministry, or wherever the Lord has positioned and placed you. When Paul was writing to the Colossian church and told his readers to put on love as a bond of perfection and allow perfect peace to rule in their hearts, he concluded admonishing them to be thankful. This won't just happen; it needs to become a revelatory Word to our lives so that whatever storm, hit, trial, adversity, good time, or tough obstacle we face, we will keep the attitude of gratitude. As we sanctify our lives daily by thanking God for all that He has done for us, we will be able to face whatever challenges come our way and not be sidetracked, moved, or shaken by them because we know that we have a refuge in Him.

I am thankful for you, the reader of this book, that you took the time and made the effort to learn more about thanksgiving. So, this is my prayer for you...

May the truth of this short book be activated daily in your life

and may the power of thanksgiving transform you
into a Giant Warrior
in the Kingdom of God for His Glory.
May your perspective of God be increased
as you see His Divine Intervention and Hand
upon your life daily,
and may all Thanksgiving, Glory, Honor,
and Praise go to our heavenly Father this day.
Amen.

About the Author

A postle Rick Ciaramitaro has been the senior pastor of Windsor Christian Fellowship in Windsor, Ontario, for the past twenty-nine years. He, and his wife Cathy, travel extensively to encourage pastors and leadership teams with a message of hope. He has earned the title "Apostle of Reconciliation" from the ministers in his city because of his passion to see the churches of Canada work in unity to fulfill their prophetic destiny. Rick oversees a network of churches and ministers called Open Bible Faith Fellowship. Rick has a dynamic gift to connect and motivate people. He has tremendous insight, which enables him to mediate church problems and generate unity.

Rick and Cathy have six children and sixteen grandchildren all serving God. Their children work in various ministries of the church and are fulfilling Pastor Rick's vision of winning the generations to Christ. He is dedicated to his family and loves that they all are working together to accomplish great things for the kingdom of God.

For more information: www.obff.com

Other Books by Rick Ciaramitaro

5 Tests of Faith

Laws of Expansion

How to Pray for Your Pastor

Order at: www.wcf.ca

Endnotes

[1] See Exodus 20:12
[2] *Vine's Complete Expository Dictionary of the Old and New Testament Words*, © 1996 Thomas Nelson Publishers, Nashville, Tennessee.
[3] See Hebrews 13:8
[4] See Acts 10:38, Matthew 4:23, 9:35
[5] See John 14:9-11
[6] *Strong's Exhaustive Concordance of the Bible* http://www.biblestudytools.com/concordances/strongs-exhaustive-concordance/